ADVANCE PRAISE FOR

50 Ways to Get a Job

"Dev's book offers fun and practical exercises for feeding your professional curiosity, examining your career journey from new perspectives, and creating opportunities to have a wonderful impact on your life. For people who see a career as a mission and every day as an opportunity to learn and grow, *50 Ways to Get a Job* is an energizing read."

—MIKE STEIB, CEO of XO Group and author of
*The Career Manifesto: Discover Your Calling and
Create an Extraordinary Life*

"Finally, a career book for a generation with nonlinear careers. *50 Ways to Get a Job* gives you the practical advice you need to build a meaningful career, on your terms. This book takes you on a thrilling choose your own adventure journey to build a career—and a life—that's right for you. I can't wait to read it again (and again, and again . . .)."

—ADAM SMILEY POSWOLSKY, author of
The Quarter-Life Breakthrough

"Through a series of compelling provocations and pragmatic exercises, Dev offers hope to a new generation looking to navigate today's uncertain job market to find a job that works on your terms.

Philosophically rich and practical, this is a must-read for anyone looking to craft a professional identity in today's complex world."

—ALEXA CLAY, author of *The Misfit Economy*

"Finding work you love can feel exhausting and futile. Dev Aujla's book offers inspiring insights and tools for navigating your career in the digital age. Whether you know what you want or you're unsure what's next, this book will support you in taking the leap toward meaning and purpose."

—AMBER RAE, author of *Choose Wonder Over Worry*

"The framework and exercises in this book will help you develop faith in your own desires, skills, and abilities so that you will not only learn to trust your path, but trust yourself."   —SUMMER RAYNE OAKES, founder of Homestead Brooklyn & SugarDetox.Me

"Everyone may take a different path through this book but the results are the same—a career you have chosen and a job you're proud of. I loved that I could turn to any page and find advice that was immediately helpful whether you're just starting or twenty years in. Dev helps makes an overwhelming subject seem doable."

—RAHAF HARFOUSH, co-author of
The Decoded Company and author of *Hustle + Float*

"This book isn't just for recent grads. It's a book of elegant strategies for getting to better, more meaningful work that I can keep on my shelf and refer to again and again."

—ANYA KAMENETZ, NPR, author of *The Art of Screen Time*

50 WAYS
TO GET A JOB

50 WAYS

TO GET A JOB

AN UNCONVENTIONAL GUIDE TO FINDING WORK ON YOUR TERMS

DEV AUJLA

A TarcherPerigee Book

tarcherperigee

An imprint of Penguin Random House LLC
375 Hudson Street
New York, New York 10014

TarcherPerigee with tp colophon is a registered trademark of
Penguin Random House LLC.

Most TarcherPerigee books are available at special quantity discounts for
bulk purchase for sales promotions, premiums, fund-raising, and educational
needs. Special books or book excerpts also can be created to fit specific needs.
For details, write: SpecialMarkets@penguinrandomhouse.com.

LIBRARY OF CONGRESS CATALOGING-IN-PUBLICATION DATA
Names: Aujla, Dev, author. | Aujla, Karim Jandev, author.
Title: 50 ways to get a job: an unconventional guide to finding work on your
terms /
Dev Aujla, Karim Jandev Aujla.
Other titles: Fifty ways to get a job
Description: New York: TarcherPerigee, 2018. | Includes bibliographical
references and index.
Identifiers: LCCN 2017033682 (print) | LCCN 2017035285 (ebook) |
ISBN 9781524705220 | ISBN 9780143131533 (paperback)
Subjects: LCSH: Job hunting. | Vocational guidance. | BISAC: BUSINESS &
ECONOMICS / Careers / Job Hunting. | BUSINESS & ECONOMICS /
Motivational.
Classification: LCC HF5382.7 (ebook) | LCC HF5382.7 .A865 2018 (print) |
DDC 650.14—dc23
LC record available at https://lccn.loc.gov/2017033682

Printed in the United States of America
1   3   5   7   9   10   8   6   4   2

BOOK DESIGN BY KATY RIEGEL

This book is dedicated to my family and is written in honor of all the jobs they have had over the hundred years since they arrived in Canada. This is the work that enabled me to be here: cattleman, pig rancher, laborer, farmer, mill worker, truck driver, secretary, store manager, server, nurse, office manager, real estate agent, property manager, brewery technician, lawyer, bank teller, artist assistant, executive director, recruiter, writer.

CONTENTS

STUCK

APPLYING FOR JOBS

INTERVIEWING

HAPPY

FOREWORD

DEV AUJLA HAS the most intriguing mind of anyone I've ever met. Sometimes we'll have a conversation and he'll say something like, "Well, I'm a little tired." Then, when I push him on why he's tired he'll reveal that he's been working nights. I'll dig further, only to discover that actually it's not work in the way I might conceive of it. He'd been manually going through a community bookstore that was going out of business every single night for a month straight, sorting out and buying books from its owner in order to start his own library. The best part is that he says it all in a way that makes you say, "Wow. That's a really cool thing. Can I come along?"

The good news is that now we can. Dev has written a book that takes us by the hand so that we can experience work with the same drive and dedication that he does. To hold this volume in your hands is to hold an invitation not only to a mind that will advise you on work in ways you may never have imagined, but also to find joy in the journey of seeking a meaningful career path. Finding a job is not about some painstaking process of looking at job boards and filling out applications online, hoping that the employer on the other end of an inbox will understand you. It's about pursuing questions, spending time with people who are genuinely interesting to you, and seeing new career possibilities in the most familiar of places. Dev has handed you the invitation—distilled into this book—that does all of those things.

I first met Dev during my own time of work transition. I had recently come off a stint as a community organizer on a political campaign. It was one of those things I did on a whim and had no relevance to my previous career in Buddhist nonprofits. I was actively trying to wrap my mind around a new venture that combined the community organizing work with my meditation training. Our conversations during this time were all about navigating our nonlinear paths, about the ups and downs of being in the middle of the unknown, and about the possibility and potential we saw as we found our way through. It was, in many ways, the same conversation that you will now begin as you work your way through the exercises presented in this book.

50 Ways to Get a Job shows us that we don't really know where life and our career will take us. They are, as Dev illustrates clearly, nonlinear. Ben Franklin once said, "When we're finished changing, we're finished." While a bit blunt, the point is spot on. You and I are constantly in transition, learning new things and growing every day. It's no surprise that our understanding of what meaningful work entails would similarly shift and morph over time. The idea of identifying a career, doing that one thing for the rest of your life, and getting a gold watch upon retirement has become a rarity. This book is the guide for a new generation of worker.

We live in a time when we need fresh thinking about how to approach getting a job, and how to find meaning in this arena, our work, where we spend most of our waking hours. What Dev has outlined here is the most holistic approach I have ever seen to finding our motivation and purpose behind work and how to get the job that is ideal for who you are right now.

This book will get you the job you want, sure. But before you dive in I have two disclaimers:

1. This book will change your life if you let it. Getting a good job, or perhaps a better way to put it would be the job that is right for you, includes changing your relationship to many other aspects of how you view your world. The book includes content on how you can best transform your home, how to change your relationship to money and your personal budget, and even how to introduce yourself at a party. This is not just another book about careers; it's a book on how to live.

2. You gotta do the work. I mean it. When I launched my nonprofit, the Institute for Compassionate Leadership, a number of years ago, it was a no-brainer that we would bring Dev onto its faculty. He introduced the 50WaystoGetaJob.com site to our students and there was a marked difference between those who thought it was cool and spent an hour checking it out and those who took the time to actually do even a handful of the exercises. Those that spent more time doing the work that's now been expanded upon in this book ended up actually getting jobs that were perfect for who they are.

If you feel stuck and want a change in your life, this is the book for you. But you have to put it down from time to time and do the research, writing, and exercises outlined within. The good news is that it's fun. It's the book we need for finding work today, and I want to thank Dev for writing it. With his unique perspective, he's the only one who could. How lucky are we to have in our hands a guide that's able to gently prod us in just the way we need to get us moving to exactly where we want to go.

Lodro Rinzler
bestselling author of *The Buddha Walks into a Bar*

INTRODUCTION

WHEN I WAS TWENTY-SEVEN, I had the perfect job at the intersection of making money and doing something good for the world. I was working for a company that stood for everything that I believed in on a small team that was responsible for business development in New York.

I was learning how to sell, and I was surrounded by purpose-driven people. The company had the mission-feeling of the nonprofit I used to run, yet we had an expense account and the resources of a growing business.

I realized that I was unhappy when I was coming home from work one day and walking up the stairs of my apartment building. I noticed that the marble was worn in the middle and there was a layer of dirt around the periphery of each stair. It had been months. Why had I not noticed this? Hundreds of times people had walked up these steps, stepping only in the middle in the exact same way. I remember thinking I was just like all these other people slowly wearing down these marble steps. I had always been someone who looked at things and wondered. I used to notice things like the steps right away and try to change my habits, but I hadn't done that. After eight months of this job, the part of me that had creativity and agency felt dormant. From an external perspective, I should have been happy, yet internally I wasn't. How could I have let myself get to this point?

I was working at a company that represented everything I believed in and yet it wasn't for me. I wanted to be having conversations I enjoyed every day, not selling people things. I wanted to be involved in listening to people, building a movement, person by person, and helping people. I knew I could do more, yet I was unsure of how everything could shift to get me there. I wanted to get back to a place where I would notice the stairs again.

Three months later, while I was still at the job, my boss called me in to her office. I was being let go. I was given three weeks of severance pay and told I was no longer needed. I left the office and walked the forty minutes to my apartment and stopped at a restaurant across the street. I ordered a salad and a glass of wine and considered where I was now. This was what I had wanted—right? I had been trying to find a way out of that job for three months, and yet I was caught off guard. How was I going to pay my rent? What did I want? Was this what it felt like to get what you wanted? Between bites I kept wavering from a place of confidence to questioning everything all over again.

In the coming weeks, I sketched out a plan. I figured out how long my money would last, I spent time describing and understanding my dream job, and I even wrote fiction about myself in order to imagine an alternative way my life could be.

I realized I wanted my everyday routine to involve going for lunch with friends. I wanted a job that enabled me to build relationships over time and be able to sit and listen to people one-on-one. It began to become clear that my next move would look completely different from what I'd imagined and that it would definitely be different from anything I had ever done before.

I spoke with one of my old mentors during this in-between time, and she said offhandedly, "There is always someone that makes money wherever money changes hands regularly." I began to make a list of situations and job titles where this was true regardless of whether a given one was something I could see myself doing.

- Real estate agent
- Business development
- Talent agent
- Partnerships
- Gallerist
- Fund-raiser
- Recruiter

Recruiting. It seemed plausible. It made sense. It had been there in front of me and yet it was something I had never done. My career had always been nonlinear—it didn't follow a set path or road map. It curved and changed in ways I would never have imagined at the outset, but once I learned to trust it, I found that it would always provide exactly what I needed.

This shift was just another reminder that it would remain that way.

I have had a lot of jobs and a couple of different careers over the past fifteen years. I have had what they call a portfolio career—projects, companies, nonprofits, freelance gigs, and normal nine-to-five jobs. I ran a nonprofit called DreamNow, and I worked at fast-growing start-ups and most recently with a venture firm in New York.

Four years ago, I ended up running my own recruiting firm, called Catalog, which now works with some of the largest nonprofits and start-ups in the country. I have now learned from both sides of the interview table. Through my work I have helped hundreds of people get jobs at companies and nonprofits that are a perfect fit for their own nonlinear paths, and I can help you too.

Now the best part of my day is when I get to sit with people, often over lunch, and listen to their stories. I hear about what work means today, about the ups and downs and realities of the job search, and I learn from them. Some people cry when you ask them how they're faring, while others will sit in front of you rattling off a preordained script. I have drawn lessons from both.

I set out to learn the real tactics behind what it took to get the perfect career. I raised more than $500,000 from foundations and spent three years with a team of others researching and experimenting with different tangible methods for getting a job.

My partners and I talked to more than three thousand people who had varying perspectives on how to navigate a career today. We talked to career counselors, self-help gurus, tech companies that run job boards, and recruiting services. We built partnerships with nonprofits that tested different exercises on university campuses. We reviewed dozens of tools, books, and resources that stretched back to the early 1970s and tracked how career advice has been offered and changed over the last fifty years. Even more importantly, I talked one-on-one with hundreds of individuals who were unsure about their next step and listened.

As a result, I came up with the idea for a simple website, 50Waysto GetaJob.com.

In a world of loose self-help concepts, I wanted to offer practical, tangible steps that would help people find their next *right* job in a meaningful career.

Two days after 50WaystoGetaJob.com launched, I woke up to a dozen text messages and e-mails. The site was down. I phoned the Web developer and the designer to tell them what was going on. The site had had tens of thousands of visitors—even news outlets had picked it up. I couldn't believe it—I knew the steps would resonate with someone, but I had no idea it would connect with so many.

We didn't set out to reinvent the job search. Instead we set out to understand people's experiences along the way, and as a result we built something people haven't stopped coming back to. All of a sudden we had all this data showing us how people navigated their nonlinear careers, showing us what they cared about most and what they came back to.

This data, combined with the countless stories that I have heard in the past two years, form the foundation for this book.

Our careers are nonlinear. We will move between industries and become employed by companies that don't yet exist. The problem is that the world is changing, and yet the job search hasn't.

The advice we get on how to find jobs is static: follow your passion, network, work on your resume, apply to job boards, and wait.

This method of finding a job leads to a consistent emotional arc—or rather an emotional nosedive—that starts the day you begin searching. The process is demoralizing and frightening for most. It is one of the reasons so many of us stay in jobs we know aren't making us happy. The average job search can take six weeks or longer, and yet it is human nature to hit an emotional low within three. From that emotional bottom, you are in your worst position to be searching, negotiating a salary, or building the skills and confidence you need to know you are worthy of a job with purpose.

There is a better way. This book represents a different approach. It is a method that gives you agency, freedom, and creativity. It reverses the emotional arc, giving you the calm control you need to leave a job you are unhappy in because you will know exactly what to do the next day.

TWO TYPES OF JOBS

There are two types of jobs that you can get. One is the type of job where you mentally check out, bide your time, and collect a paycheck. In this job your days are filled with a type of work that often feels stressful, frantic, or meaningless. The second type of job is filled with the kind of work that feels natural, that comes easily, that rejuvenates you, and that isn't motivated by stress or fear.

To understand the subtler differences, consider for a moment the work it takes to melt a ball of snow by holding it in your hand. There *is* work being done. Your body is doing the work—your heart is pumping warm blood through meters of blood vessels. Simultaneously your nerves are letting your brain know your hand is cold, to increase the supply of blood to that region, and as a result of the rush of blood to your hand your skin warms, and that heat transfers to the snow and it melts.

This is all happening effortlessly. You are holding a handful of snow, and as you take a deep breath in, the work is done and the snow melts.

That is natural work.

There is another way to melt a handful of snow. You can walk inside, open a cupboard, and find a steel pot. You place the pot on the stove, put the snow in the pot, and turn the gas on. You wait for the metal to slowly heat and then the snow melts. You turn the burner off, rinse the pot in the sink, dry it, and return it to the cupboard.

There is work in both. The kind of work and the kind of job this book will help you get feels like the former. The kind of job that is as natural as a deep breath in and out.

This book has a hidden curriculum—it will teach you a way of approaching the job search that is grounded in asking questions, sustaining inquiry, listening deeply, and knowing yourself, all so that the process can be less of a chore and more of a natural progression. It gives you a calm directionality that will stay with you throughout your career.

For years, we have viewed our work and life as separate. The methods that we use to consider or improve the way we live would never be applied to the more structured career side of our day. As our careers have become less linear, this separation has faltered and the thinking we have been using for the past three decades is no longer working.

This book is aimed at helping you recover from a life broken into separate compartments. As you explore one exercise focused on the way you live, you will find something shift that will transform how you work.

THE NONMAGIC WAY OF GETTING THE JOB

We are taught that after an hour of work you will see an hour of results. This isn't true when it comes to our job search. Hours of work and meeting people may lead to nothing, and then everything changes with one meeting, one e-mail. There is no right way or correct timeline with which to navigate our careers.

In his book *The Experience of Insight*, Joseph Goldstein explains the feeling I felt when I first understood this nonlinear way of viewing progress and the mind-set you will need to adopt when starting your search. "Hasten slowly," he says. "Hasten in the sense of being continuous and unrelenting in your effort, but do so with poise and equanimity. Persistent and full of effort, yet very relaxed and balanced."

Not everyone succeeds in getting a job or experiencing this feeling. Some people would rather pay others to do the work of figuring out their life for them, or they will spend hours searching for magic shortcuts instead of developing the practices that will last a lifetime. We all want to believe in magic—we want to believe it is possible—but if we think something happens by magic, it is often simply that we're not seeing the real work that was put in.

In a special I was watching on the street magician David Blaine, in one of the vignettes he lets us see behind the scenes into his year-long process leading up to one trick. In the segment he travels around the world to track down a stranger he saw on the internet who could teach him a physical feat that involved holding liquid in his stomach and ejecting it with fire-hydrant-like force and volume. He spends a year training himself to be able to physically do this, and then more time with a team that choreographs and rehearses the performance elements of the trick that is centered on this feat. And it's all for only two minutes of a show with some forty people in attendance.

The magic for those in attendance is the two minutes: the buildup and the grand reveal. But when you see the process—the months of work, the plane trips, the training, the research, and the scripting of the trick itself—the magic disappears. It is a sure thing. Of course he can do it. He worked for it. Magic is the erasure of work. It is what we want to believe is possible.

Only once in a while do we get a glimpse of the reality, the work behind something that seems magical. The narratives that we most often read about people's career paths are magical. They follow a prescriptive form—point of inspiration, purpose, an obstacle overcome, and emergence at the top of a field.

The nonmagic way of getting a job is less stressful than hoping for something that doesn't arrive. If you want to claim a skill on an application you need to actually find a teacher, learn the curriculum, practice, and gain that skill before you can check the box. You have to put in the work. In Matthew Frederick's book *101 Things I Learned in Architecture School*, lesson 33 is, "If you wish to imbue an architectural space or element with a particular quality, make sure that quality is really there. If you want a wall to appear thick, make sure it is thick." You could just check the box without the effort, but you miss out on what happens along the way, which is where the best jobs are found.

The path in this book is a sustaining one that isn't based on magic. It puts the choice in your hands, so that you're no longer reactive and waiting for the next big opportunity but actively creating, living, asking, learning, and moving toward the career you deserve.

HOW TO USE THIS BOOK

The fact that you picked up this book means that you have made a choice to pursue a new path and are already well on your way, in the middle of your journey. Whether you are actively looking for a job or you are happy in the one you have but want to be prepared for what happens next, this book is here to help you.

There is no right path through this book. We need different steps at different times, and you are the only one who knows where you should begin. Many of the exercises relate to each other, and throughout you will find page numbers in parentheses that direct you to other exercises. Finish reading the page you are on or take a choose-your-own-adventure approach and turn right away to the next exercise.

The only thing that will ensure that this book doesn't work is if you don't put the book down once in a while. If you don't do the work it takes to speak with people (112), to consider what you actually want (31), or to search for answers in unlikely places (90), you won't end up with the job you want.

The exercises in this book weave in and out of the practical and the philosophical. They sometimes contradict each other, but that is on purpose. There isn't one right answer when it comes to our careers. Challenge yourself to stretch your way of thinking and do the exercises that feel a little uncomfortable.

The book should be treated as a malleable guide that invites you to adapt the exercises and ideas so they work for you. If you come to a point where you feel like you know the next step without help from the book, you are doing it right. Congratulations.

The exercises are organized in specific stages: starting, finding your purpose, overwhelmed, learning new skills, networking, stuck, applying for jobs, interviewing, and, finally, happy. They are emotional, and you can move between them within the course of a day. Ask yourself how you feel, where you are in the job search today. And then turn to the section that speaks to you most.

The process of finding a job and navigating these exercises has been designed as a cohesive whole. Some of the fifty exercises featured in this book, like being aware of your commitments (59) or noticing your personal gravity (27), are practices that you have to remind yourself of consistently and that will serve you long after you have gotten your ideal job.

The act of finding a job should feel the same as the job itself—an engaging experience that has purpose and direction. It should be filled with wonder, possibility, and the conviction that there is a path forward and that meaningful, real work is not only possible but it can start now. So let's begin.

STARTING

MAP YOUR CURRENT CAREER PATH

You are already in the middle of your career. Even if you have never had a job before, you have learned, had experiences, made choices, expressed interests, and here you are deciding where to go next.

To truly understand this requires you to spend time looking backward to map how you ended up here. A beginning can often feel like a cold start with zero momentum. It can be overwhelming, and in a state of panic you may end up on job boards—the last place you should begin (167). You deserve a better beginning that honors your path so far, that is informed by your past and builds on what you have learned.

Mapping your career path to date will help you identify trends, patterns of feelings, and reasons for transitioning out of and into work, insights that will inform your path through this book.

In his bestselling 1980s career book *Transitions*, William Bridges breaks down the stages of a transition. There is an end, a period of in-between, and a beginning. Each stage is essential yet rarely considered in a distinct way. As you review your map, pay attention to your moments of transition and pause to consider how you navigated each stage in those moments.

What were you ending? What were you beginning? What did you

have to let go of in yourself at these times? What beliefs did you have to change and what external changes followed? Do your transitions always follow a place-based change, or do they follow a change in belief? What did you think you were going to gain in the next stage? What ended up happening?

The arc of your career is part of a broader story.

Let's zoom back out, and as you review your map take note of broader patterns, industries, themes, and clues that could inform your next step. Ask yourself: What do you want to repeat? Do differently? Learn from? What industries or potential jobs emerge that may have been hiding in your peripheral vision? Right before you got your last job what did you feel? Did you listen to your gut, or did you force yourself to change? What are you moving toward? What are you escaping?

THE EXERCISE

Begin mapping your career by following these steps:

1. Make a list of fifteen different milestones, relationships, people, jobs, or experiences that brought you to where you are today.
2. Create a map with your milestones. Connect them chronologically, noting the impact each had on your state of mind at the time. Draw your map on a whiteboard or a large piece of paper.
3. Pick two random points and try to add five more milestones, people, or experiences—no matter how small—that got you from one step to the next. Repeat as necessary to fill in gaps in your map.
4. Choose a different pen color and note your emotions throughout the map. How did you feel before and after you got your last job? When did you last feel overwhelmed or totally satisfied?

WHAT'S NEXT?

→ Go on a solo trip and spend time in reflection (40)
→ Find a friend in a similar situation and share your career map (6)
→ Make your own finish line and mark an ending (139)
→ Make a list of what you want to learn next (72)

FIND A FRIEND
IN THE SAME SITUATION

THIS IS A JOURNEY that is best done together. Having a partner will help you solidify what you've learned along the way, reflect back the boring moments, and open you to a whole other experience of navigating the next steps in your path.

Find someone in the same situation as you. Whether you have both outgrown your current job or you share the same job title, make sure your shared context is the same. The ideal partner could be someone you work with, an old friend you haven't connected with in a while, or a new one you met at an event (122). This person doesn't need to be a best friend. It can be someone on the periphery, someone you've unexpectedly opened up to about your career and you want to get to know. Feel free to stretch yourself to find someone new; buy them this book or send them to the website.

Do it together.

The benefits of starting this transition alongside someone who is also going through it are innumerable. This friend will hold you accountable, give you momentum, and help you overcome that initial inertia needed to make a change. The things that we want most can be the hardest to do. Your partner for this journey will be a pressure valve—

someone who can listen if you need to vent anxieties or share what you've learned, someone to help you fend off disappointment and celebrate victories.

You will take different paths through the book. No matter how similar your situations, you will each build your own way and outgrow this guide at different times, finding your own answers and developing your own methods. By working together, you benefit from double the conversations, double the insights, and double the network.

Get together once a week. Notice as you work through the book which exercises you have an aversion to or feel will be hard to do. Talk about those together and commit to doing one each. Pay attention to the voice in your head saying "I don't need to do that." These are the exercises you should discuss and decide to tackle with each other's support.

THE EXERCISE

1. Choose someone who is in the same situation as you.
2. Commit to a weekly meeting for six weeks.
3. Make a commitment to each other to do a number of exercises in the book, taking particular note to discuss the ones you innately want to skip over.
4. During each meeting, share any advice you received and review the people you met that week. Go over the exercises you both completed and compare notes.

WHAT'S NEXT?

→ Send a "looking for a job" e-mail to five close friends (143)
→ Practice different ways of introducing yourself (126)
→ Make a list of twenty people whose careers you admire (99)

SCHEDULE A
VACATION BUFFER

WHEN WE HAVE BEEN WORKING in one way for years and we decide to change what we do each day, our old way of living re-creates itself unless we are aware of this pattern. Our brains and our bodies have been taught to move and operate in a specific way, and our natural inclination is not to disrupt it.

When looking at a lineup of Olympic athletes, we can see their different areas of expertise through the shape of their bodies sculpted by their hours of training and practice. Our work and daily routines similarly give shape to our minds. We naturally want to continue moving in the same way we have been. If our jobs are stressful, this could result in a default tendency to re-create this same stress.

If we want something different, we need to begin to move a different way. This shift can feel uncomfortable at first. A vacation buffer is an active acknowledgment that a transition is happening. The exercise has one essential component and it is of particular importance for those who have been in their careers a long time, the seasoned athletes of their field: take a break.

Begin by acknowledging that it won't always feel comfortable to completely change your everyday way of being. If you structure your days in your work life, try to take a vacation with unstructured time. Stretch yourself and feel the shift. Keep yourself out of the office long enough that you settle into a new rhythm.

This rhythm isn't the permanent rhythm for your life (alas, it doesn't include work), but what's important is that it's different. Notice how long it takes you to get comfortable with a new rhythm. Consider what is easy about it and admit what is hard. What do you find yourself re-creating from your old patterns? Stay as long as you can in this transition space.

A vacation buffer is a liminal space, an in-between. It is a period to recognize endings and holds open the possibility of what's to come next. Don't rush to fill your time. During the course of your vacation buffer consider what rhythm you want to have in your next job, what your life demands of you now, and what is possible now that you know you can change.

THE EXERCISE

1. Choose a date and set a timeline for your trip. The closer you can plan a vacation buffer to the actual end date of your job the better. It will help demarcate the change.
2. Choose a place based on whether you want to combine your vacation with purpose by going on a solo trip (40), traveling to a beach, or clearing your schedule to stay at home. The important thing is to plan activities that are different from what you would normally do.
3. Track how you feel throughout the trip. What is easy and what is hard about this new rhythm? What do you find your mind going back to consistently? These observations will help you figure out how to adjust your rhythm when you get back home.

CHANGING YOUR SPEED

Different stages of life demand different rhythms, different paces. There are great career decisions to be made whether life demands you have to speed up or slow down. Major life experiences such as having a family, moving to a new country, or working through grief all demand a change of speed and accepting these changes does not mean sacrificing ambition. When you accept a change in pace you are able to act from a place of strength that results in less struggle and less stress. Here are three steps you should take when considering a rhythm change.

1. Investigate an Old Rhythm
   What was the rhythm of your last job? What is the speed of the life you want? How do these two overlap? What was the experience and feeling of living with a different rhythm like?
2. Map the Changes
   What factors have changed in the past six months that demand a new pace? Changing your speed begins with accepting these new facts and seeing them as a foundation of strength. Be sure to note both external and internal factors. What rhythms do you want to continue? Should the pace of your life speed up or slow down in response to these changes?
3. Identify Stepping-Stones
   You don't have to adjust all at once. Identify stepping-stones that you can use to re-create some of the qualities of your old life and provide a bridge toward the new way you want to live.

WHAT'S NEXT?

→ Learn about how your center of gravity affects your decisions (27)
→ Practice a new method of taking notes (86)
→ Reconnect with five mentors from the past (112)
→ Make a list of your skills (69)

DOWNLOAD YOUR
BANK STATEMENT

ROBERT GASS, a leadership coach whose work is grounded in Buddhism, says that "stress is resisting the reality of what is happening." He explains that the world is what it is whether we acknowledge it or not—it is the act of resisting that causes our anxiety. This realization shifts the responsibility back onto us—we're the ones that must look, accept, and see it for what it is. Although this may be true, it is still hard to put into practice. For example, it's hard to make yourself sit down and look at the reality of financial information you don't want to see.

At various points throughout your career there are times when you don't have the resources you need, and in those moments it is more important than ever not to ignore your financial reality. This exercise can be used to get any information that you need that you have been ignoring— be it a test result, feedback on an interview, or, in this case, a bank statement.

To overcome your resistance, begin with scheduling something that you really want to do with a friend. It can be as simple as lunch, but it must be with someone you enjoy spending time with and who is readily available for a last-minute plan. Schedule it for later today or tomorrow.

Fifteen minutes before you leave the house, put on your shoes and be ready to go. But instead of walking out the door, walk to your computer. Now is the time. You're all set to head out the door, but instead you sign in to the bank website and download all your bank statements from the last six months.

Begin looking at them and start to figure out how much you have and where you have been spending money. Find out whatever the information is that you have been ignoring. You have to rush, as you have someone waiting—but make sure you begin looking. Maybe you need to categorize the expenses from the last month to figure out what you are spending on, or maybe you need to see how much you still owe on your student loan. This exercise works for any information you are avoiding looking at. This is your chance to get that information. You know what information you've been ignoring.

The rush of just doing it will give you about twenty minutes of momentum—there won't be enough time to really figure out what it all means, but before you know it you will be scrambling, wanting to continue, and then you're already five minutes late. You have to leave.

Go. Leave the house. Leave the work on the table.

Now you are with your friend doing something that brings you joy, all the while knowing this information you didn't have before. Enjoy the meal. The world hasn't ended. Now you know. There is a slight sense of relief. Remind yourself of the quote—"stress is resisting the reality of what is happening." You no longer have to resist. Your task has changed to simply figuring out what to do next.

The mental anxiety of not knowing is one of the worst types of anxiety. It paralyzes. The fictions that fill the gap between reality and your imagination are never good ones. This is especially true when it comes to your bank accounts, your debt, your money. This "rushing through it" trick works because the alternative—opening up the letters, downloading the bank statements, and then being faced with an endless amount of time to contemplate the decisions that got you here—is much worse.

Rushing isn't resisting—it's embracing. This exercise will give you just enough momentum to come home and easily approach the information that you left midstream and continue to figure out what it all means. The hard part is already done. You simply have to continue what you started. Momentum is on your side.

Whether you discover that you have only a week's worth of resources left or six months' worth is neither good nor bad. It is simply important knowledge to have that will help you figure out what steps to take. It will help you decide which of the "ways to get a job" you should do first. At the end of this section, I have created a list of the different chapters that are especially worth considering based on whether you have less time or more time.

THE EXERCISE

This task is about gathering and analyzing your financial information. You don't have to make any judgments, changes, or decisions. Just do the following:

1. Make a plan with a friend that you know you'll enjoy.
2. Fifteen minutes before you have to leave, put on your shoes and get ready to go.
3. Now download your bank statements.
4. Before you leave the house, quickly go through the last three statements, classifying your expenses into categories like food, entertainment, life necessities, and cash.
5. Find the information that you have been avoiding. Begin analyzing it.
6. Leave just in time to meet your friend and follow through with your plan.
7. Come home and finish off your analysis with the momentum you created by starting this exercise earlier in your day.

DETERMINE YOUR RUNWAY

Once you have your bank statement and know what your financial situation looks like, you have to determine how long your money will last. This length of time is called your runway. Do the following steps to figure out your runway:

1. Analyze and categorize your expenses into "necessary" and "nice to have" and plan two monthly budgets assuming a short or a long runway.
2. Weigh each option, considering your current job prospects and your comfort with risk. Do you want to leave yourself a long runway, or are you confident that you will find a position within a month?
3. Choose a runway and budget that you feel good about. Make sure to include some room for unexpected events by making it a little bit longer than you expect and then commit to this.

Once you have made the commitment to your chosen budget, release yourself from worrying about money and concentrate on following the plan you made. If you chose a three-month runway, commit to not thinking about your bigger-picture financial situation until the end of the first month. Then you can take stock and figure out how you are doing, notice if there are any adjustments you can make to how you are living, and record where you strayed and where you stayed true to your budget. Did you under- or overestimate your comfort with risk? Don't judge yourself—just adapt based on where you are now. This type of thinking removes the everyday pressure of worrying about finances that can be paralyzing, enabling you to be clearheaded for your job search.

WHAT'S NEXT?

EXERCISES FOR A SHORT RUNWAY

→ Make a list of what you want to learn in your next job (72)
→ If you feel overwhelmed, apply the tenets of "Everyday Prozac" (47)
→ Create a list of companies you want to work for (119)
→ Send a note to friends telling them you are looking for a job (143)
→ Get a side hustle to extend your runway (180)
→ Practice living with less (162)
→ Write this e-mail to a company you want to work for (184)

EXERCISES FOR A LONG RUNWAY

→ Write fiction about yourself (37)
→ Choose three events to attend (122)
→ Create a company brief about a company you are interested in (78)
→ Make some changes to your living space (50)
→ Start capturing and recording the articles you read (108)
→ Spend time learning to ask better questions and cultivating curiosity (133)

UPDATE LINKEDIN AS YOUR FUTURE SELF

YOUR LINKEDIN PROFILE is one of the first things that a potential employer sees. Starting your search by refreshing your profile as a version of your future self is as much a signal to future employers as it is a signal to yourself that you are moving on to a new stage of your job search.

Your future self is the idealized version of who you want to be gathered from stories, role models, magazine articles, and lifestyles you've come across and admired. Be warned: If you were to update your LinkedIn profile as your future self without reading any further, you run the risk of both lying and turning your profile into a mood board. This may help you get an interview but not the job.

If this exercise feels daunting and you don't know yet who that future self is, then skip this chapter and return to it later. Instead spend time finding a just-ahead mentor (148), writing fiction about yourself (37), or building your course pack (108).

This exercise should feel exciting—start with that mood-board-esque dream life you defined (31) and, over the course of an hour, work your way backward until you arrive at the next-step version of your future self. The goal is to find a version of you that is one step forward from where you are today. Sometimes the shifts are subtle ones, such as highlighting two extra skills that you are developing, or sometimes it involves reframing your headline from your last job title, to something more general, such as "operations for start-ups." Other times the shift you make involves leaving something out, thinning out a description, or retelling an aspect of your past in a way that better fits the narrative that connects you to your future self. Your LinkedIn profile does not need to be the definitive tell-all version of yourself—it is a very particular story and you have the right to include what you want. These acts of revision are about crafting, editing, and taking control of your story. You don't have just one fixed identity; you don't have to announce each change publicly—you can just change it, make the shift, and tell yourself and the world a new version of your own story.

The next-step version of your LinkedIn profile is the in-between story that connects your future self to your current self.

THE EXERCISE

1. **Walk backward from your future self.**
   To discover those small changes and quarter turns you need to make on your profile, walk backward from your future self and write the story that got you there. Pay particular attention as you approach the present day. What changes, shifts, and quarter turns do you need to make? One way to do this is to revisit your nonlinear career map (3) and highlight milestones that support your future self and downplay those that confuse the narrative.

2. **Change your profile picture.**
   Changing your picture signals that you are ready for something new.

3. **Change the description.**
   Change the description of what you did in your last position in a way that sets you up as the perfect person for what you want to do next. Not sure what that is yet? Describe your dream job (31).

4. Omit information.

Omit information like a certain profile description, a given skill, or a past job that doesn't propel you toward your future self.

5. Endorse new skills.

Get one or two friends to endorse skills that you are beginning to build and reorder them so they appear closer to the top of your proficiencies list.

6. Add contacts.

Take an hour to review everyone you know on Facebook or in your e-mail contacts and add them on LinkedIn.

WHAT'S NEXT?

→ Revisit your career map and look for trends (3)
→ Interview someone who had a linear career (34)
→ Find a mentor who is a few years ahead in his or her career (148)

FIELD NOTE:
DEALING WITH JEALOUSY

As we scroll through our lives on our phones the feelings of jealousy, of missing out, and of not having our lives figured out can be paralyzing. These feelings are always magnified during times of transition, especially when comparing ourselves to the high-gloss version of people's lives on social media.

In order to deal with this in a way that actually addresses it instead of masking it, we have to rethink the systems we live our lives by.

As you do the exercises in this book, you will make adjustments to how you live, your routine, the way your home is laid out, how you take notes, and more, all to have the effect of making your life singular, unique, and immune to feelings of jealousy. Each of the elements that you change is a system you use to govern your life. Changing these systems directly changes what you interact with and what you feel on a daily basis.

Systems don't need to be complicated. A system can be as simple as a single question. At the heart of Marie Kondo's bestselling book *The Life-Changing Magic of Tidying Up* is the question "Does this spark joy?" If something in your life doesn't, you get rid of it. If it does, you keep it. Her question is the whole system. Consciously choosing and adapting the systems you use every day helps to build a resilience to feelings of jealousy. Once you have a structure of your own that suits you and your needs, you won't feel like others have something you don't.

Let me tell you about two cases where people have taken this type of thinking to an extreme. The first is the artist Donald Judd.

Donald Judd was a minimalist artist who was prolific in the 1960s. Today, his studio is run by the Judd Foundation and is part museum, part archive, restored and frozen in time from when he lived, worked, and entertained in the building. He bought the old industrial building in SoHo in the 1960s, and he transformed it over the decades into his ideal work/life environment—each floor having a distinct and separate purpose: eating, entertaining, working, sleeping.

The space was customized to suit the exact way that he lived. There was nothing extra—two small closets that perfectly fit the number of coats he owned on the sleeping floor, a table that had a secret compartment so that he never had to see the china, an Ethiopian headrest and Japanese tatami mat laid out next to his working area so he could smoothly transition from painting to resting in the middle of his workday. The space was at times cold and hard to imagine living in—it was clear that it was built for his way of living. To be anyone else in that space would be incongruous. It was a physical system of living where everything had been considered, from the singular chair in the library to the industrial pail used as a garbage bin. Everything fit the aesthetic and, more importantly, addressed his emotional needs.

Casa Luis Barragán in Mexico City is another example of a system of living that was built with precision. Luis Barragán was something of a playboy in the architecture world. His own house was his life's work, constantly under revision, slowly built to perfection—for him. Barragán loved riding horses; it was where he experienced the height of happiness. On the top floor outside his bedroom, there was a small room where he stored his riding gear. There was a simple bench against a wall, and across from this bench was a staircase with a yellow glazed glass door at the top. Every day at the exact time that he would sit down on the bench to put on his riding boots, the sun would pour through the glass door from above, casting a yellow stream of light onto him as if it were God himself blessing him as he prepared to ride. This was typical of the Barragán house. Each moment and each place was a choice. It was considered and purposeful and structurally set up to reinforce the values that he lived with.

Both Barragán and Judd took the principle of building a system of living to its limits, spending years building and perfecting their spaces so that they reflected and enabled the ideas and emotions they wanted to feel at any given moment. The structure and physical system in which they lived reinforced their values and aesthetic. It made their lives singular and unique to them.

Most of us don't have the time or the money to rebuild our houses so that each unique space serves an emotional purpose. But even without making grand gestures you have the power to begin to build a system and change the structure of your life and physical environment (50). Your systems require making a choice. They demand that you choose and know what you want. There is no moment, routine, or problem you face in your day that is too trivial to consider as a worthy place to enact these types of choices.

When I got back to my apartment from touring Donald Judd's studio I was excited at the possibilities of what it would mean to build a system in my apartment that would enable me to think and feel what I wanted throughout. I wanted to clarify my thinking and have my home be as suited to me as Judd's studio was suited to him. I made a dozen small changes that weekend, from moving photos around so they'd help me think about the right things at the right times to repositioning furniture for the ideal sun exposure based on the time of day that I liked to sit in it. The biggest change was painting my radiators white. I took the afternoon and painted all of the dark silver radiators in my apartment the same white as the walls—it transformed the visual field when I walked in the door. The radiators disappeared and the room felt clearer and more open. It was a subtle change, but it gave me more room to think. My apartment was becoming mine.

Later that week, I was invited over to a colleague's apartment in the

West Village. It was beautiful, two stories and well furnished. It was one of those apartments that I normally walk into and face a whole cascade of feelings—mostly jealousy. Should I have this? Should I move? Am I enough? But this time something else happened.

I sat down with a glass of lemonade and all I could think was that this wasn't for me. The radiators weren't white. There was no jealousy or runaway inner dialogue. I immediately noticed all the ways that this system of living wouldn't have worked for me—it was just a different apartment.

There are hundreds of small choices you can make that extend beyond your physical space into the ways you choose to interact with money, friends, time, and even jobs. By taking ownership of how you behave in relationship with these things, you take power out of those feelings of jealousy. Your life is unique by choice. My friend who travels and works on the beach in Bali is living a different life—this friend has built a system different from mine and made different choices. When you do this, it becomes easy to understand your life as confidently your own. This is the strong, grounded foundation you need to survive social media today so you can remain confident and find, interview, and get your ideal job.

FINDING
YOUR
PURPOSE

FIND YOUR CENTER
OF GRAVITY

IMAGINE FINDING A JOB that fits perfectly with the way that you naturally are and the way that you interpret the world around you. Finding and understanding what your center of gravity is will help you achieve just that.

Your center of gravity is a characteristic tied to the way that you experience what happens to you. It is neither a good thing nor a bad thing. It simply exists, and we all have our own. It is a quality that helps you interpret your reality—and oftentimes it can be at the root of why you transition in and out of jobs.

My center of gravity revolves around being liked or loved, and it affects everything in my life. I think about people all the time—whether they will like me, how my communication will be received. Until I identified this and became aware of it, I would worry about something, such as waiting for a mentor to respond, even though the person had given me no reason to be concerned, and I could spend hours reviewing old communications, wondering if I'd done something wrong. This was my center of gravity at work bending the reality of the situation, making it seem more important than it was. Your center of gravity has control over you until you name it and become aware of what it is.

After explaining this concept to a friend of mine, I took a guess that her center of gravity revolved around being right. She always needed to prove that her opinion was right. The next day we were having lunch and she said, "It is being understood. You think it's me being right, but it's being understood." She then proceeded to give me examples that ranged from when she fell in love with her current boyfriend to when she got to give her opinion at work and have it heard and she felt deeply rewarded. Being understood was always a central part of these experiences. It was her gravity.

A nurse I interviewed explained how her center of gravity was being in control. Nursing was generally more of a caregiving profession, but throughout the course of her career she had found her way into a job in the critical care unit, where the nurse needs to be most in control, commonly dealing with acute situations.

Uniqueness, being alone, authenticity, acknowledgment, and feminine power are all examples of centers of gravity from individuals I've interviewed. It can be anything—and often those closest to us can tell us what ours is.

In order to identify what yours may be, consider the following circumstances:

- Think about the last three times you got overly upset in a way that was disproportionate to the reality of the situation. What were the reasons why? Do you notice any similarities between them?
- We often build systems and complicated beliefs that help us manage our center of gravity. We may find relationships that counteract or feed into this quality. What center of gravity has shown up in your relationships? Have you made adjustments to your life based on your center of gravity?
- Think about multiple moments when you have argued against or stood up for something with passion. Is there a center of gravity at play in these moments?
- Make a list of major decisions you have made in your life or at

moments of transition. Look for patterns of potential centers of gravity that may have influenced the decisions you made.

⊓ Ask family and friends and have an open conversation about what they think your center of gravity might be. Although they may get it wrong, their thoughts may point you in the right direction.

Once you know your center of gravity, things will shift. You'll start to notice it at play in even the smallest of situations. When I first realized mine, I started making a "gravity log" on my phone, jotting a small note each time I felt like I was making a decision that was influenced by my desire to be liked or loved. I then asked myself a key question: Is this serving me well right now?

My career had actually been built to benefit from my center of gravity. As a recruiter, I was the center of a wide network of people constantly navigating competing interests, getting clients and potential candidates to like me, to think about me, and to ultimately connect with each other. Doing my job well was helped by my natural inclinations. The inverse was also true. There were times when it wasn't serving me. Knowing when it wasn't "reality"—when it was just my center of gravity at play—enabled me to let go, not worry so much, and move on.

There is no right or wrong center. By identifying it, and noticing when it is at play, we relieve ourselves of the stress of having to change it. We can simply choose to ignore it when it isn't serving us and even find careers that benefit from our natural inclination.

THE EXERCISE

1. Using the list of questions and suggestions above, spend time learning about your own center of gravity.
2. Now test your center of gravity. If you were given two choices, one that played into your center of gravity and one that didn't, which

would you choose? Would this always be the case? Talk to friends and family and get their opinion after sharing the results of your exploration.

3. Create a "gravity log" by making a note each and every time you notice your center of gravity influencing a decision you make. Each time you make a note, ask yourself, "Is reacting this way working for me in this moment?" If it is not, choose to ignore your impulse, trust that it is coming from your center of gravity and not the reality of the situation, and make a different decision.

4. If you don't actively consider it, your center of gravity forces you to naturally prioritize certain behaviors and decisions over others. What kind of career could benefit from this kind of sensitivity and prioritization? If you care deeply about being seen, for example, then maybe you should consider professions that naturally require you to be in front of audiences. What social situations or workplace scenarios would actively benefit from your natural way of being? Add these to your list of ideal careers (99) and identify potential companies where this career would be possible (119).

WHAT'S NEXT?

→ Write your own job description (200)
→ Make a list of job titles that would benefit from this new understanding (176)
→ E-mail someone you don't know (115)
→ Record yourself in a stressful situation (152)

DESCRIBE YOUR DREAM JOB

Now is the time to embrace your daydream. This is the moment when you channel the electric excitement that comes from imagining limitless possibilities and fill in the details and subtleties that transform that thought into a clear picture with you in the center.

Here are three questions that will help you bridge the space between the idea and the reality. If you don't ask these three questions in succession, you may be able to describe your job, but you won't be able to fully visualize the life you have when you get there. These questions, which I first wrote about in the book *Wanderlust* by Jeff Krasno, work together and enable you to envision a future that doesn't require you to trade your life for your work.

1. **What do you want?**
   Make a list of everything you want in life, including material things and money. Where do you live and what do you want your home to look like? What kinds of relationships do you have? What are the material things or experiences that you imagine will bring you happiness? It is normal to feel resistance when answering this

question because money can matter a lot or not at all (212). Lean into any discomfort and answer as truthfully as possible.

2. **What path do you want to walk?**
   This question is rarely asked with as much depth as the first, yet it is the key to your happiness. The path you want to walk is the process by which you will get what you want. Do you want to have time for family and friends? Would you like to have long days or short days? How do you want to spend your time? How does creativity fit into your day? If you don't ask this question, you will default to the easiest and most visible path to get what you want. For example, if you want a lot of money, you might become a banker. Later on in life you may come to the realization that you really don't enjoy what the life of a banker entails. By asking yourself about your path at the outset you can avoid wandering down the wrong ones and be more comfortable with changing it if necessary.

3. **How can this path help you get what you want?**
   Our brains are wired to synthesize and make sense of disparate information. By asking how your path can help get what you want, you will begin to see answers that you didn't realize were possible. The critical voice in your head might say, "Well, that's not realistic. You can't make a lot of money and have free time. Reality works like *this*, not like *that*." This voice will keep you on the easiest and most visible path and does not have your best interests in mind.

People accidentally trade their quality of life (or ideal path) for what they want because they mistake the most readily accessible way as the only way to get something. When we look around, we can point to many examples—models, people, or case studies—that seem to prove that taking that readily available path will lead to the thing we want most.

However, if you answer the questions above in earnest, the answer to the third question—how that path can help you get what you want—may not lead to the fastest journey. It will most likely not be the easiest.

Often it will require you to look hard for role models and cobble together stories that make that sense of possibility a reality.

But it is possible. Harder, but possible.

Our lives aren't just our work. We change during the process of getting what we want, so we owe it to ourselves to choose what we do each day—to choose the path that we want to walk. Some decisions really test our commitment to this—decisions where we are offered the salary, the fame, or whatever it is we really want in a way that is clearly misaligned with the way we want to live. Pay attention to these. There is a real power that comes from recognizing and turning down these opportunities. If you have the chance to make a decision like this—celebrate it.

WHAT'S NEXT?

→ Go to a job board to look for your dream job and then immediately leave (167)
→ Find your future boss (130)
→ Revisit and make changes to your LinkedIn page (17)

INTERVIEW SOMEONE

SOMETIMES YOU WILL FEEL ALONE during the job search. You will feel that your particular set of circumstances, the things you've learned, your specific time pressures, and your experiences have no parallel. You are right. They don't. And yet there is comfort in understanding someone else's unique path. We don't often get the unedited version of someone else's story. When we read about people's stories or when we ask offhand, we usually get a simplified linear version that explains how people got to where they are today.

People aren't trying to hide the truth; people often simplify their stories because they assume that most people don't want to know the complicated and often conflicting reality of a nonlinear path. People make their paths linear through omission—the active choice to leave out the half-considered opportunities, the extenuating life factors, the moments of unknown, of weighing competing interests, and all those times they say no to opportunity without knowing yet what the next thing will be.

Your job is to interview someone with the goal of uncovering their real story. This is as much an act of reassurance as it is an act of discovery. You will uncover choices you may be able to apply to your own career, and you will deepen your relationship with the person you are interviewing, and both of these things combined can lead to introductions, better questions, and even job opportunities that you may not have recognized regardless of how dissimilar your interviewee is from you.

People appreciate being given permission to be honest and tell their story. This is not an informational interview. You are not trying to learn about their job. You are trying to complicate their linear narrative—to seek out the nonlinear. Fashion yourself as more of a journalist with the goal of uncovering truth rather than an eager job seeker.

Be curious and encourage them to slow down and go a little deeper when you sense major transitions in their story. Even the most linear paths rely on chance meetings, the right conversation at the right time, and competing life circumstances that are rarely shared—it is your responsibility to be open enough to see it.

THE EXERCISE

1. Choose someone whom you imagine has had a linear career trajectory or simply a "regular job."
2. Ask to interview this person about his or her career path.
3. As this individual shares his or her story, explore what chance occurrences, run-ins, or meetings led the person toward this particular path. Use the following questions as prompts and ideas to help you develop your own:
   - What options were you considering before you made that decision?
   - How did that particular transition come about? What were the circumstances that led you to know you were making the right decision?
   - How did you feel before you made that career move?
   - How did you end up meeting the person who got you the job? What enabled that relationship to develop the way it did?

- ◆ Was there a moment when you thought you were going to do something different? What pulled you in the direction that you eventually ended up going in?
- ◆ Did you know that the outcome of that decision was going to be a job? What did you think the outcome was going to be? What was your plan if that had been the case?

4. As this person's story reveals itself, play the role of the journalist or writer seeking to add as much color to the story as possible. Include as many details as you can remember.

WHAT'S NEXT?

→ Follow up on something that you learned by structuring a research trip (75)
→ Work on complicating your own story by writing fiction about yourself (37)
→ Discover other ways to build your mission alignment (194)
→ Organize your job search in a spreadsheet (170)

WRITE FICTION ABOUT YOURSELF

WE ALL HAVE ONE PERSPECTIVE of our lives, and the longer we have been pursuing our career, the more solidified this view can become. But the truth is, we all have other lives that are possible, that lie just under the surface—parallel worlds where we made different decisions, where we built other skills, chose to live in different cities, or stumbled into different careers.

When you stretch your thinking beyond what you know today and allow yourself to imagine alternative lives that might be, you open yourself up to the serendipitous connections that happen across different story lines both real and imagined. Writing fiction gives you permission to consider an alternative story of your own life.

Ashish had been working at an innovation consultancy and in the agency world for more than ten years, and when we sat down together I could sense he was expecting a normal recruiter meeting where I'd pitch him the next logical step at a competing agency. It was clear to me that there was something else to talk about, and that he was wondering if he ought to stay on this same track. He was open to considering an alternative future. We began talking about his fictional possibilities, and the energy in the room shifted. Ashish's fictional reality transported him to a career where he was directing a film and working in creative marketing with human rights organizations and could spend time with his daughter.

Fiction has the power to break us out of the regular patterned way we see ourselves. It helps us create room for careers and opportunities that we wouldn't see possible in any sort of traditional planning exercise. How you react to that fiction can be just as telling as the story itself. It can enable you to take a leap of faith, which can be hard to do when you're examining yourself. It is indulgent, necessary, and sometimes exactly what you need when you feel stuck in life or limited by what you have done before.

THE EXERCISE

1. Begin by making a list of real milestones and experiences from your life. Include any resources you have, such as your home, or a skill you've already mastered, and be sure to add anything that showed up on your nonlinear career map (3).

2. Add ten fictional milestones as bullet points anywhere on the map. Choose things you have never done. Things that excite you. Challenge yourself to imagine something completely fictitious, not just a path you didn't take.

3. Now comes the creative part. Consider all of these points as a whole and write three alternative stories of your life. Omit bullet points that are true or add in fake ones to build a completely different bio, one you would have never previously considered. Write a future biography for each story line. What did this fictional character end up doing? How did this character achieve his or her goals?

4. As you look at these alternative biographies, consider what it would mean to actually pursue these paths. What skill would you have to learn? What city would you have to move to? How could the current realities of your life actually help you move into one of these

fictional futures? What would you have to let go of? What would this new path enable or change?

5. Reflect on the implications of these stories and questions on your own life.

WHAT'S NEXT?

→ Consider switching career paths completely (158)
→ Find a new community of people while you learn something new (82)
→ Look for answers to questions your fictional writing raised in unlikely places (90)

GO ON A SOLO TRIP

I HAVE ALWAYS HOPED that I would be one of those people who would experience a grand epiphany that would give me purpose and direction. My first solo trip was the perfect cinematic place for this grand realization—a national park off the coast of Vancouver Island. The epiphany didn't end up happening, and yet it ended up being the best way to get the clarity I needed to take the next step in my career.

You don't need to be a hiker or an outdoors person to take a solo trip. Find a cabin or an Airbnb rental and just be somewhere by yourself. You may go camp in a forest far away from everyone, spend some time writing and reflecting, and nothing will happen. That's okay. That's the point. Actually, do it and trust that not all progress can be measured or noticed right away. I can guarantee you that you will be two or three days closer to getting a job after returning from your solo trip because you will be clearheaded, grounded, and ready to make important decisions about your career.

I met Kevin through a program called the Institute for Compassionate Leadership. He and his colleagues were some of the first people to use the original 50 Ways to Get a Job material and try it out in their moment of transition.

Kevin was two months away from finishing his master's program in landscape architecture at the University of Washington. He was not a camper. The last time he had done anything remotely close was when he camped at a music festival—and he was definitely not solo there. What ended up pushing him out the door for three days was a mix of wanting to prove to himself that he could do it and the novelty of experiencing something he'd never done before.

He took his little 50 cc scooter and drove four hours to the farthest, most northwestern point of the continental United States, a place called Cape Flattery in Washington, and set up camp for three days.

Kevin was beginning to transition out of the school mind-set, trying to figure out how to actually be a landscape architect. He knew that a job search was supposed to be about waking up every morning, logging into a job board site, and sending out a dozen applications for anything that was remotely related to his field—but it just felt like a vacant lottery with a high chance of losing or getting a job you didn't want.

After setting up his camp and unpacking everything he had crammed onto his small scooter, he spent the next three days wandering around, taking photos, walking through the forest, and eating oatmeal.

When he arrived back at his apartment in Seattle, a subtle shift had occurred. When he explained it to me he said, "The solo trip was what enabled me to step out of the context of Seattle, take a breath, and look at my career and see that the work that I wanted to do couldn't be done there—or if it could, it would be more difficult. Stepping outside, walking around, and getting that perspective really did give some sort of movement toward my decision to move to New York."

There was something intangible about leaving the anxieties of the city and his routine for just a few days that introduced the idea to make the move. Within four months of moving to New York, and after an unexpected turn during the interview process, he landed his first job out of school as a landscape architect intern with the City of New York Department of Parks and Recreation.

You can't force realizations. Changing where you sleep, what you eat, and how you spend your time for a few days will be enough to change your mind-set. You don't need to force it. Find your own catalyst that will push you out the door. If you don't want to deal with cooking, give yourself permission to get in your car and drive to a restaurant. If you don't know how to set up a tent, rent a cabin. Just make sure you are somewhere without others, ideally surrounded by nature and totally different from your current setting.

There is no right way to spend time alone. Just get out the door, don't expect anything to happen, but know and trust that you will be a few days closer to getting a job.

THE EXERCISE

1. Plan your trip. Set a date for a solo trip where you bring nothing other than a notebook, food, and water.
2. Abandon your connection to the outside world and leave all your technology behind. This exercise only works when you are truly disconnected, so you must leave your phone behind (or at least keep it turned off).
3. Stay at least three days, or as long as it takes to quiet your mental chatter. Do all of the thinking that you came prepared to do and then stay one day longer. In this extra day you will receive the gift of mental space, which you cannot prepare for or find any other way.

WHAT'S NEXT?

→ Try a new decision-making method (205)
→ Decide when to work for free before you are asked (197)
→ Reintegrate into society by choosing three events to attend (122)

FIELD NOTE:
FINDING A NEW WAY OF BEING

TIMES OF TRANSITION are the ideal moment to reinvent yourself and try on a different way of being. If you are a frenetic person this is an opportunity to be calm. If you are outgoing and are naturally the center of the room, a transition can be an opportunity to feel what it means to sit back, listen, and watch. You can use the momentum of change in your career to try different ways of carrying yourself, of acting and thinking. Mimicking a new way of being can help you see other types of job opportunities you would have never noticed if you were your normal self.

I once took an afternoon workshop on tracking animals in the wilderness in the mountains of Utah. The guide had grown up tracking and had spent years traveling around learning from different indigenous elders. He explained to us that when he was sitting with the elders and they began talking about a particular animal, they would instinctively start moving like the animal they spoke about. They would be talking about noticing the trail of a snake and their hand would naturally move in serpentine waves mimicking the animal's movements.

Our guide explained that mimicry actually unlocks a different form of perception, and he got us to try. We were all huddled around a small dip in the forest where water had gathered, and he instructed us to embody a deer—to move around the area stooping to the same height and walking as we imagined a deer to walk. I bent over, curved my shoulders upward, and led myself head forward through the light brush. Immediately I understood and started to notice different things: fresh buds that had been nibbled and branches that had unnaturally broken a few feet below my normal resting gaze.

Imitating others—animals or humans—can help us notice new things, subtle behaviors, ways of responding, speaking, or talking. Imitation is one of the tools that we have to help us understand a new way of being. Empathy is linked to imagination, and the act of pretending enables us to access a new form of knowledge. If someone tells you to act calmly, you may re-create a caricature of a calm individual in your mind. But when you decide to embody a calm person, to take the time to mimic one, the gestures and behaviors are more subtle and more empathetic.

As you try different exercises throughout this book, you have an opportunity to try on different ways of being. The goal is not to trick yourself into being a deer, or being a calm person by acting like one, but rather to notice a few new behaviors or feelings that you actually do want to integrate into your life. By actually enacting these small gestures, you remove the need to tell people you are a certain way. Your actions speak for themselves, ensuring that the person you want to be is the person you live and act like and not just the person you talk and post about.

OVERWHELMED

COMMIT TO DOING THESE FOUR THINGS WHEN YOU FEEL OVERWHELMED

LOOKING FOR A JOB is stressful. It's easy to spiral into doubt and to self-sabotage, losing all momentum. An effective cure for feeling totally overwhelmed is what I call Everyday Prozac.

When searching for a job, you may know mentally that you are doing the right work, and yet you may still find yourself frustrated or empty at the end of the day. Everyday Prozac, when practiced for a week, helps you weather the temporary ups and downs of a nonlinear path that are actually a signal that you are close and that you're doing the right thing.

Our bodies are locked into a conversation with the way we feel. They react, they echo, they speak, and sometimes the conversation gets needlessly elevated, making it hard to hear what we actually feel. Everyday Prozac de-escalates the conversation your feelings have with your body. It gives you what you need in order to listen to your body again so you know when and if you actually do need to change the rhythm or shift course on your path. Even if the moments when you feel grounded are temporary, they can still be the best times for you to make big decisions.

This exercise is about finding a path to those moments so you relieve yourself of the pressure to make any decision when you're overwhelmed. Here's how it works. If you are feeling stressed, angry, frustrated, hopeless, jobless, or otherwise out of sorts, don't act on any of these feelings until you:

1. Sleep for seven hours (or whatever a full night's sleep is for you)
2. Eat a full, healthy meal
3. Exercise
4. Treat yourself to something you love

Any negative feelings you have, regardless of how rational they may seem, can be given no credit, time, or mental space until all four of these things are completed. Create a list of things you love and store it away so that when you are upset you can pull the list out and quickly pick one.

If you do all four things listed and you still feel depressed, hopeless, or angry, you have my full permission to wallow, cry, phone a friend, or change course. Commit to this practice for one week and see what happens.

As with any new system, you should feel free to adjust it so that it speaks to you and works for you. It is important to remember the intention of this exercise. The purpose is not to dull your feelings or escape from them, but rather to create the physical, emotional, and mental space that will allow you to hear what is going on inside and listen to that voice.

Challenge yourself to come up with one additional activity that you want to include in your version of Everyday Prozac. Ask yourself, "What activities give me the mental, emotional, and physical space to feel grounded?" It is important to write this list when you least need it. Trying to think of things that make you happy when you are sad can be hard. If you're feeling down at the moment, stick to the core list, and don't worry about adding your own activities.

THE EXERCISE

1. Make note of when you are feeling stressed and overwhelmed and write it in a notebook. Don't judge yourself. Simply begin by noticing.
2. Commit for one week to the four core principles of Everyday Prozac; use them whenever you notice that you are stressed and before you act or make a major decision.
3. When in a grounded and calm state, make up your own form of Everyday Prozac. Apply as needed.

WHAT'S NEXT?

→ Help five others in your network (102)
→ Situate yourself and find a sense of calm (63)
→ Reconnect with a friend who is in a similar situation (6)

MAKE STRUCTURAL CHANGES TO YOUR LIVING SPACE

THE PHYSICAL SPACE you inhabit can be a source of clarity and rejuvenation. During the job hunt, this is more important than ever. It can mean the difference between remaining motivated and clearheaded going into an interview and second-guessing yourself and setting off an emotional dive. This exercise will help you ensure that your environment is refined for your use. That way, you can find your way back to your most grounded self even in the inevitable moments of stress in a job search.

Regardless of whether you live in a studio apartment or a house with acres of land, your home holds innumerable opportunities to make structural changes beyond those aimed at providing comfort and practicality. The goal of this exercise is to help you consider how a space can make you feel and how to make changes that bring about the ways of being that you want to embody. Space can make it easier for you to live the way you want.

Walk around your home and stand in different places. Stop in the spots where you normally do daily activities—putting on your shoes, making breakfast, even brushing your teeth. Now ask yourself in each specific place: What do you want to be thinking and feeling during that activity?

How could the spot where you sit when you put on your shoes before heading out remind you of what you want to feel before you go out into the day? Like Barragán drenched in light as he put on his riding boots (20), how could you change the lighting or change what is in your line of sight so as to conjure a new feeling?

These decisions are all about choice. Let's say one choice you make is to eat less food from the microwave. You currently own a microwave, there is room for it, it's paid for, and it has its place in the kitchen. After making the decision to use it less often, most of us would leave it there reminding ourselves of our commitment each time we wanted to heat up food. Instead get rid of the microwave altogether and you will never have to make the decision of whether or not to use it. The easiest option becomes the one you desire, to heat up your food without a microwave. This is what it means to work on building a system for your life.

A decision to structurally change something so that you don't use the microwave may seem like a small and meaningless thing to focus on, but making it easier to make the right decisions helps you gain clarity. The act of perfecting these small decisions strengthens your sense of agency, so when the moment comes when you are asked to write your job description (200) (which is an opportunity to structurally change your workday), you will naturally know what to do and how to ask for what you need to deliver on exactly what you promise.

Consider and make these changes throughout your home. On the days that you aren't feeling particularly mindful, you will be sitting down to put on your shoes and you will look up and see the photo you hung up on the wall. You will have changed the physical structure of your home so that your mental response becomes the ideal one.

In his book *The Portable Coach*, Thomas Leonard, who was one of the pioneers in the personal coaching industry, offers one exercise that approaches these small structural changes in a different way. This exercise is grounded in the idea of considering tolerations. Leonard explains that we all carry with us hundreds of things that we tolerate—small annoyances that aren't large enough to warrant attention and that are small enough to live with on a daily basis. It may be a zipper that always gets stuck or the fact that we always run out of toothpaste.

His exercise is simple and transformative—fix all your tolerations. Try it. Make a list of everything you tolerate and dedicate one day and $150 to structurally changing these things so you will never have to deal with them again—get a new zipper on the jacket, buy a year's supply of toothpaste, and so on.

You likely won't realize the weight you've been subconsciously carrying around until you experience the alternative. Once you restructure your home, you will experience a new kind of freedom. This freedom helps you counteract a sense of feeling overwhelmed, and it will enable you to find the clarity and mental space you need to make important decisions during your job search.

THE EXERCISE

1. Walk around your home identifying three to five places that you interact with on a daily basis.
2. Consider how you could change the space to ensure that you feel or think in a way that creates your desired mental or emotional state.
3. Make a list of all your tolerations. These could be as simple as a broken zipper, a strap that irritates you on your backpack, or always running out of hand soap.
4. Dedicate one day and $150 to removing all of your tolerations.

WHAT'S NEXT?

→ Tackle something you have been avoiding, like downloading your bank statement (12)
→ Consider the balance and roles of physical and mental work in your life (187)
→ Prepare your personal story so it is interview-ready (191)

SIT QUIETLY IN A ROOM FOR FORTY-FIVE MINUTES

DURING THE JOB SEARCH you have to deal with many competing voices and ideas and the pull between reality and dreams. The act of sitting quietly is an act of trust. It allows the ideas in your head to find unsuspected connections.

A couple years ago, I had the opportunity to cohost an hour-long session for thirty-one students at a conference at Columbia University. They came to the talk expecting to learn how to raise money and momentum for their social enterprises. After my usual introduction, I shared the following quote:

> Man's number one reason for unhappiness is his inability to sit quietly in the room.
> —*Blaise Pascal*

I then repeated it slowly—the number one reason for unhappiness is our inability to sit quietly in a room.

I told everyone that we were going to do something different and I invited them to put down their pens, put their cell phones away, and join me in sitting quietly for the next forty-five minutes.

I sat down and stared straight at the clock at the back of the room. Five minutes went by. I felt hesitation combined with a "what is this guy doing?" attitude in the air. I sat through it. Fifteen minutes later the first person walked out. In the next five minutes another seven left the room.

Twenty-three people remained. At that point a remarkable feeling settled into the room. Everyone seemed to take a breath and rest into a comfortable and sustained silence for the remaining time.

After the forty-five minutes were up, we opened up the discussion and I asked the group what they'd learned and what they thought about the experience. Time had moved slowly for some and quickly for others. For some there were grand insights and others felt nothing more meaningful than a few moments of reprieve. People had connected the session's proposed topic, "raising money and momentum for your social enterprise," with the act of sitting quietly in amazingly inventive ways. They talked about the connection between feeling grounded and centering oneself during the tumult of raising money. They talked about patience and connected the exercise to the importance of self-confidence. The conversation turned to the personal practices we need to adopt in order to remain grounded and do our best work.

The only ones who received no value from committing to that forty-five minutes were the ones who left.

THE EXERCISE

1. Set an alarm for forty-five minutes. If you are using your cell phone, put it in airplane mode. Turn off all other electronic devices.
2. Get a notebook and pen. If something critical comes to mind that you don't want to forget during the forty-five minutes, quickly jot it down but make it brief and quick. This is not a writing exercise. Write only if it is absolutely necessary.

3. Get comfortable.
4. Take a deep breath.
5. Begin.

After your alarm goes off, pause and reflect on what this exercise has to do with your current approach to your job search.

WHAT'S NEXT?

→ Learn to delay gratification by finding interest in the details (94)
→ Win over someone who cast you aside (155)
→ Determine how much you need to make (212)

RETHINK YOUR DAILY ROUTINE

WE ARE PATTERN-BASED CREATURES. We do the same thing most days. There is comfort in routine. It helps us make sense of large amounts of information. Routines create order, and in times of chaos and tumult, when our routines are forced to shift, the feeling of being out of control gets magnified. Rethinking your daily routine will help you remain calm when overwhelmed and help you start living the life you want right now.

A new routine can be as simple as getting coffee in a new way. Whether you change the time, the route you take, or the method you use to make it, the important thing is that you choose with intention, building a daily routine that makes you feel grounded and confident.

I met a woman named Kari Betts who had a unique view into reliance on routine in times of transition. She worked for a private company that provided a combination of career center services and shared working spaces for people who'd been laid off from large companies. She was there during the height of the financial collapse and she saw hundreds of ex-bankers and ex-lawyers who were getting laid off come through her doors. She spoke about how intensely these recently laid-off individuals clung to old routines, arguing over office space or coming in at exactly 8:05 a.m. even though their reality had changed drastically.

If you don't actively choose your daily routine in times of transition, you'll just re-create what you had before. The momentum a new routine offers you will help you feel less overwhelmed and can be something that you carry forward into your next job before you even know what it will be.

THE EXERCISE

1. Figure out what your daily routines look like. Notice how they shift once you commit to making a career change. Which routines have you lost and what new ones have you gained? Are there routines that you can rethink or perform in a new way that honors how things have changed?
2. Rethink three of your daily habits or rituals. What do you want to feel? How can this ritual help you feel that way? What can you change in your daily life that will make it easier to follow through on your new daily routine?

WHAT'S NEXT?

→ If you need a more drastic change, schedule a vacation buffer (8)
→ Learn to take better notes (86)
→ Start work without telling the company (209)

RENEGOTIATE FIVE COMMITMENTS

WE ARE CONSTANTLY making small commitments, to ourselves and to others, that we sometimes don't even notice. Some people accept it as a part of a busy life—overcommitted and overwhelmed, running from one thing to the next, trying to follow through. If you want to have the mental space to deal with the uncertainty of navigating your job search, you need to become aware of this and renegotiate your commitments regularly.

We rarely consider that we can even do this. I used to think about commitments as either those that we delivered on or those that we didn't—success or failure, a pass/fail test. Then I began to notice the commitments that fall into a perpetual purgatory—the endlessly delayed ones, the bottom of the to-do list, the ones that I would say I would get to but never did.

These are the commitments you are going to renegotiate. Renegotiating them can feel hard to do, like you're admitting failure or letting people down. Clearing your commitments will be immediately gratifying and will create free space you didn't even realize you were missing. Here are a few tips that can help you confront the reality of your situation and negotiate your way to a clearer mental state.

• *Focus on what you are saying yes to.*

Saying no to one thing is saying yes to something else. Saying no is an act of prioritization. Our priorities shift as we gain experience and learn more information. Reground yourself in today's priorities. What will saying no to these commitments enable you to do? How would it feel to make an active choice that proves you are prioritizing the things you want in your life?

• *Lower expectations and practice surprise and delight.*

Sometimes the expectations people have of you prevent you from even starting. Release yourself fully from a commitment you've made and rid yourself of all expectation; then, without telling the people you're working on it (very important), give yourself the chance to surprise and delight them by following through anyway. After you've reset expectations to zero, anything you do will be seen as a positive.

• *Talk about what you've learned.*

Instead of jumping straight into the renegotiation, start the conversation by talking about what you have done so far and what you have learned as a result. This could include the complexity, the time it takes, the amount of resources, or the challenge the commitment poses. Sharing what you've learned is a good transition point in the conversation to renegotiate the commitment. This is an opportunity to both give real value to the person and explain why it is that you have to renegotiate.

• *Make the pain of not doing anything large.*

Consider what happens if you simply never do something you're supposed to at work but don't let your boss know. Imagine you did this for all of your commitments. What would that do to your reputation? What would it mean to do a really bad job on the commitments you made because you are too busy? What would happen to the relationship then? And on a more personal level, what would happen to your health if you carried the stress of unfulfilled commitments for years? If you recognize that the pain of leaving things in limbo is worse than the temporary pain of having an honest conversation, renegotiating your commitments becomes easy.

THE EXERCISE

1. Write down five commitments that you have made to either yourself or other people. They can be big or small, but choose the ones that are weighing you down the most. Start with the commitments that have remained at the bottom of your to-do list for weeks.
2. Tackle them one at a time. Phone or e-mail the people you made the commitment to and tell them that you have to readjust the promise you made. Either explain that you can't deliver and you are sorry, or renegotiate for more time, more money, or a different outcome. Release yourself from at least two of the five commitments.
3. Now that you have a fresh slate and a clear mind, start a commitment notebook (see below) and experience the magic that happens in the next week as you record all the new commitments you make to yourself and others.

KEEP A COMMITMENT NOTEBOOK

Recording your commitments will train you to notice the small promises and eventually help you to cut down on unnecessary ones. You will build momentum, which will naturally help you with the larger commitments—like getting a job.

Carrying a commitment notebook to record any commitments you make to yourself or others has two immediate effects that you can only fully understand if you stick to it for a minimum of two weeks: first, you make fewer commitments, and second, you become hyperaware of how you phrase things to others. Wording is the difference between promising to send a book to someone versus telling them to look the book up on their own. It is also the difference between running into a colleague and saying, "I am so glad we got to see each other," versus, "I can't wait to see you next time—let's get lunch soon." These are subtle changes that normally go unnoticed but add to the background ledger in our minds.

1. Buy a small notebook and carry it around with you for one month.
2. Write down every commitment you make to either yourself or someone else, regardless of how small it is. Include even the smallest promises like, "I'll send you that article," or "I'll call you next week," or "I am going to the gym today." Write down every single one.
3. At the end of the day review the commitments in your book and ask yourself if there is a way to commit to less.
4. Refer back to your commitment notebook when you create your daily to-do list and follow through with every single promise.

WHAT'S NEXT?

→ Reassess your budget and financial runway (12)
→ Win over someone who cast you aside (155)
→ Consider your current balance between physical and mental work (187)

FIELD NOTE:
SITUATING YOURSELF

It is easy to get so immersed in our everyday experiences that we lose perspective on where we are in the longer arc of our lives. We forget where we are physically, beyond the room we're sitting in, the city we live in, and the country we are a part of. We can lose track of our place in history and forget just how long people have been experiencing the same emotions.

The feeling that situating yourself brings can be helpful whenever you get too overwhelmed, too caught up in how important each meeting and each decision is. The process of situating yourself is an act of grounding. It is an act that slows you down. It helps you understand time and scale. It is a pause that brings you up and out of yourself and the stresses of everyday living so that you can feel calm and realize how little control you have and that the world will continue regardless; and in accepting this logic there is hope and reassurance. Knowing where you are situated ties you to a history of people who came before you who have wrestled with similar questions with fewer resources, and despite this they have figured out how to sustain themselves. It is a grounding realization.

I once signed up for a two-week workshop at Arcosanti in the middle of Arizona. Created in the late 1960s by the architect and philosopher Paolo Soleri, Arcosanti bills itself as an "urban laboratory." Soleri built prototypes in the desert for alternative ways for people to live, a new model for an urban environment.

Roger, our facilitator, had been there since the beginning. He had built much of the place with his own hands, alongside thousands of "workshoppers" over the years. He started our workshop by drawing mountains on the whiteboard in front of us. He explained the meteorological conditions governed by where we were and the soil and how it changed with the altitude. He explained that we were surrounded by two mountain ranges one hundred miles to either side, that they used to be as large as the Himalayas, and that we were in the middle on a plateau created from sediment that had blown and run off the mountains. He explained that three rivers flow south through the state and then connect with the Gila River, which drains into the Colorado River and eventually ends up in the Gulf of California. He walked us through the plant life, the trees, the geologic events, and the anthropologic history of where we were.

It gave me a sense of comfort to know where I was, to know that there was logic behind the weather patterns, that the mountain ranges a hundred miles away on either side held me. That people for thousands of years had been here and continue to be here. A sense of place. When we live in cities we can forget to look beyond the buildings to the broader environment and context that we live in.

If you feel stressed at any time throughout this book stop and ask yourself where are you right now. No matter how busy you are, take ten minutes or an hour or a day and make it your mission to find someone local to explain and give you context for where you are. Here are some questions to begin asking:

- Describe the physical landscape within five hundred miles of yourself.
- Understand how water travels from where you are standing to the ocean. What rivers does it travel to and where does it end up?

- Who were the first peoples on this land? What was their culture and how did they live in relation to the same landscape you live in?
- How did languages develop in this region? Did they travel up from the south or across as people moved west?
- What shapes the seasons here? What is going on meteorologically? Why is there a warm breeze or heavy and short rains in March?
- What plants grow here?

Situating ourselves in a context helps us realize that we are here in the middle of a vast landscape pursuing an arc that started in the past and that will continue beyond us. We see that where we are is a natural place to be. There is a logic to the place, and this logic not only makes us feel less overwhelmed but may hold insight into what we should be doing next.

LEARNING
NEW SKILLS

MAKE A LIST
OF YOUR SKILLS

EVERY CAREER ADVICE BOOK tells you to make a list of your skills. There's a good reason for this. It is a simple exercise that we often think we know the answer to, so we don't bother doing it. We don't take the ten minutes or half hour to find a quiet place and actually ask ourselves: What are the skills that I have?

Take the time right now and make the list in your notebook. Really, do it now.

The skills at the top of your list are usually the ones that you have been recognized for.

I was once on a walk with a friend who had gotten fairly involved in the adult summer camp world (yes, it is a real thing!), which is characterized by the love of play and a detachment from work and technology. She asked me a question that came from her camp experience: If I were an animal, what would it be? I responded, a fish. She asked me again, and said I couldn't respond with the same animal: What kind of animal are you? I responded, a turtle. She asked me a third time: What kind of animal are you? And I thought about it and I chose a whale. Back to the sea.

She then broke down my responses for me: the first time I responded was how I see myself, the second was how the world sees me, and the final animal I chose was how I truly am. I actually felt good about my animal choices and found some truth in her analysis.

The skills you identify for yourself function in a similar way. It's useful to ask yourself three times. Your first list represents the skills you think you have. These are the skills that you may have already put to work in your past jobs.

Now try again: What skills do you have? Make sure you don't repeat any of the skills from your first list. Set a watch and give yourself five minutes.

These are the skills that others see in you.

Now for the third list we are going to deviate from the animal analogy and instead of uncovering some deep truth dressed up as a giraffe, I want you to consider some of the following questions as you attempt to build your skill list:

a. What skills are you using when you feel filled with purpose or content?
b. What is a skill from your past that you have forgotten about?
c. Think about a series of different places: your favorite place of inspiration, a place from childhood, workplaces where you thrived, places where you exercise. For each of these places ask yourself what skills are best expressed there.
d. Name skills tied to physical feats, mental feats, or your intuition.

These skills aren't any more true than the ones above, but rather they may be long-forgotten skills, they may be seldom recognized, or maybe they're skills you are just beginning to explore.

Neither a job nor career resiliency comes from having the most skills. Your next job will come from being judicious, having one or two skills that you own, are proud of, and are excited to continue to work on. If a skill that you are excited about doesn't appear on one of your lists, then add it. And if it doesn't appear because you are still learning—you are ready for the next exercise: make a list of skills that you want to learn (72).

THE EXERCISE

1. Ask yourself: What skills do I have? Write down whatever comes to mind quickly. Do this for five minutes.
2. After reviewing this list ask yourself again: What skills do I have? Include a minimum of five more skills that weren't included on the first list.
3. Answer the questions outlined in the exercise above, being sure to add any additional skills that surface to your list.
4. Look up skills inventories online and add any skills that you may have forgotten. One caution to note when using these lists as a tool for self-reflection is to be aware of the tendency to overselect skills hastily, adding those which you could imagine doing. Instead, as you consider each skill, think of a time when you clearly used it—if you still want to add it, do. If not, pass it over.

WHAT'S NEXT?

→ Write a list of skills you would like to learn (72)
→ Find a job title (176)
→ Write your own job description (200)

MAKE A LIST OF WHAT YOU WANT TO LEARN

WRITING DOWN WHAT YOU WANT TO LEARN can be a powerful way to orient your next career move and make sense of a wide variety of options. With a comprehensive list in hand, you will experience an immediate sense of direction. You will have a purpose and an endless amount of new work to do.

A few years ago, myself and two colleagues, Julian Caspari and Chris Kang, embarked on a research study mapping the shifting patterns among millennials in the workplace funded in part by the Ontario government. The research involved a meta-analysis of the relevant literature, focus groups, and a wide-ranging set of interviews with both employers and millennial employees. A simple idea emerged as a result of this work: individuals were making learning-based career decisions instead of stability-based ones. People often left a company when they felt they had learned all they could there. When deciding between two jobs, they asked themselves which would offer more learning opportunities and propel them further along in their careers.

Learning-based career decisions are common in places like academia but are now becoming more prevalent in mainstream industries. We all have a learning-edge, a topic or skill that we are drawn to explore, and it evolves with our careers. Our unique learning-edge is central to how we envision what we do next.

So what happens if you choose your next career move based on what you want to learn next? The opportunities that come as a result are unexpected and can fill you with purpose. There is an emotional strength that comes from having a list of things you are excited about learning. Even the smallest learning goals can infuse your job hunt with drive and passion. Creating a to-learn list may help you discover companies that you would have never considered working for until you realize they may be the best place to check off items on your list. Your list can also be a way to decide what to prioritize.

Creating your to-learn list starts by noticing the questions that come to mind throughout your day. Carry a notebook and write them down. They can be meaningless, simple, philosophical, or something to explore on the Internet later. Why do you see mirages? How do you scale trust? How do you change the way media companies sustain themselves? There are no wrong questions. Some questions have more energy than others; they are the ones your mind returns to again and again. Others are satiated with a quick Google search or disappear when you change locations.

Your to-learn list does not need to be limited to employable skills or industry knowledge. Jobs can be courses for any type of learning—social, personal, or professional. Add to your list by considering the skills your just-ahead mentor has (148), your list of twenty companies and the skills they may require (119), or the ideas hidden in your course pack (108). Be as exhaustive as possible, adding everything you can.

The people you meet and the companies you identify as you delve into any of the questions, skills, and insights that you want to learn more about could become your future colleagues and employers just as excited and driven as you to live at their own learning-edge.

THE EXERCISE

1. Make a list of fifteen things you want to learn. Include social, professional, and skill-based knowledge. Be as specific as possible and stretch yourself to include items that will feed your whole self and not just your work self.
2. Consider other skills that your just-ahead mentor may have (148), being sure to add to your list any that resonate with you.
3. Prioritize your list items.
4. For each item, make a list of the different types of environments where you could learn this skill. Include companies, specific jobs, educational institutions, apprenticeships, and other experience-based learning opportunities.

WHAT'S NEXT?

→ Plan a research trip (75)
→ Ask yourself what companies would enable you to learn the most—add these to your company list (119)
→ Look for answers and ways of learning in unlikely places (90)
→ Ask a mentor from the past for advice on learning items on your list (112)

GO ON A RESEARCH TRIP

A RESEARCH TRIP is the perfect way to build mission alignment (194) or to sharpen a skill on your to-learn list (72). It is distinct from a solo trip (40), which is about inward thinking. On a research trip, you are going outside yourself. It is about widening your perspective, bringing in new information, and venturing toward the outside world.

A research trip has little to do with the overall results. It is about the experience of pursuing a question and opening yourself up to meet new people along the way.

It is about directionality. The word "directionality" has a sense of hope, of forward momentum. The word itself doesn't claim any direction is the right one. It simply expresses motion. On a research trip you need directionality. You are building momentum.

When I started exploring the idea of opening up an independent library, I took an unexpected research trip to Cuba. A friend had phoned me to let me know she was planning on going to Cuba and had found $200 round-trip tickets. I booked. As the date for our departure neared, I began investigating ways in which I could make my four days there into a research trip for my goal of starting a library.

I began by researching libraries in Cuba, and after finding only a little online I decided that I would make it a priority to visit the Biblioteca Nacional and to follow my instinct when I was there.

We arrived at the library without any particular plan other than to make the journey, to explore, and to take some photos. As we entered the library, a guard approached us and told us that we were not allowed to be there. He pointed us to a kind, middle-aged Cuban woman who told my friend that foreigners weren't allowed to wander around the library unsupervised. There were public tours, but it would take planning to arrange. She let us wander around the first floor, where there were card catalogs and a small gallery that featured some highlights from the library's collection of propaganda from the revolution.

We spent some time looking around. I opened the card catalogs to browse the collection and a guard approached. Not for foreigners. I had forgotten how controlled and politicized information could be. How important the simple act of organizing and cataloging was.

Research trips rarely end with insights that you'd expect. They don't need to. The excursion to the library ended up taking only two hours out of the four-day trip. I did eventually get my independent library off the ground (more on that later), and an article I wrote from this trip led to the creation of a small journal the library would publish. Research trips can be catalysts and enable you to discover new projects, and following such a hunch may even lead to a new career just like it did for a woman I met named Roopa.

Roopa was a business professor at a college in Canada and had reached a plateau in her career. She had become a business teacher by default when she was asked to take over a teacher's assistant role and it eventually led to a full-time job. She wanted a change. She decided to take a year off and launch a structured research project on alternative models of education to explore the field she wanted to move into.

The year unfolded differently from her expectation. It included mapping eighteen different educational models around the world. She conducted interviews, wrote blog posts, and created a video series about alternative education. She created a website and spent the second half of the year sharing what she'd learned with educators and her future peers and colleagues. It was an entrance to a new world and, thanks to all the people she met and work she did that year, it set her down a new career path.

THE EXERCISE

1. Even the simplest questions can lead to unexpected insights when filtered through the lens of a research trip. Choose one question to focus on throughout your trip. Consult your to-learn list (72) or consider a question from your notebook (86). Choose one.
2. Whether it is a trip you already have planned or a specific place related to your question, decide on your trip destination. There is no need to travel far.
3. Research as much as you can before you go on your trip. Look for historical examples of how people have answered similar questions. Get informed about the place you are visiting—maybe even consider looking up possible restrictions if you happen to be visiting a library.
4. Once you arrive at your destination, take notes. Pay attention to the people you meet. Interview people. Ask your questions and be open to whatever information you find. Research trips often take unexpected turns—go with it.
5. Share your results with your friends and your peers. Take the time to synthesize and understand your results and record any new questions that arise. Sharing your results is a great opportunity to reach out to someone on your list of people whose careers you admire (99) or to a future mentor (115).

WHAT'S NEXT?

→ Map the network of people you met on your research trip (105)
→ Send this e-mail to the company you want to work for (184)
→ Record yourself in a stressful situation (152)

CREATE A COMPANY BRIEF

SOMETIMES WE THINK we know a company based on its reputation, but we rarely do a deep dive into what it is really about. For this exercise you can choose any company that piques your interest. It may be a business from your company list (119), a company where your just-ahead mentor works (148), or simply one where you like the logo. Choose one. You are going to do a deep dive to try to understand as much as possible about how the company operates. This involves peeking under the hood and really understanding what it does, what it offers, who works for it, where its people come from, what direction they are going, and anything else that you can learn.

We rarely perform this level of investigation on a company before joining. However, uncovering this information can help you build mission alignment (194) and it can help you speak from a place of authenticity when you write the e-mail that will get you the job (184).

If you were an investor investing a full year's salary into a company, performing this level of due diligence would be standard—it would be your fiduciary responsibility. Although you aren't investing your money, you are certainly investing your time, and you should apply the same amount of rigor and analysis to the process of investigating which company you want to join.

Investors do this type of investigation on dozens of companies before they select the one they invest their money in. You should too.

Here are some introductory questions you should try to address during your personal due diligence process. This list is meant as a starting point—follow your curiosity and try to answer any new questions that arise as you learn more.

What is the stated mission and vision of the company?

What does the company offer or sell? How does this align with its vision?

What are the most profitable areas of the business?

How is the organization structured internally?

What is the culture of the organization?

Who are its competitors and how is what it has to offer different?

What direction is the company going in and what is the vision for future products?

Where do employees typically go when they leave the company?

Where do people work before joining the company?

What does the media say about the company?

How is it funded? Is it financially secure?

What does it typically pay?

There are a number of ways to seek out and gather this information. You can search online on sites like Glassdoor for employee reviews and salary info. For public companies, look up their annual filings with the SEC or the regulatory body in the country where they are listed on the stock exchange. These regulatory documents can be intimidating, but the risk factors section of these documents can provide you with a good perspective on what challenges the company is aware of and how the business operates. You can also approach people directly at the company, preferably middle managers who are rarely contacted with specific questions. Send a version of the e-mail you would send a future boss (115), and ask for a few minutes to talk. Contact former employees with a short note asking for twenty minutes to get a reference on the company they used to work for. Any means is fair game.

This exercise focuses solely on the act of collecting information. It will help you fill in any holes in your knowledge so you can make an informed decision on whether to invest your time, resources, and effort.

THE EXERCISE

Over the course of your job search, attempt to do this exercise on as many companies as possible. This will help you uncover hidden opportunities and deepen your understanding of the industry that you want to join.

1. For now, choose just one company to begin doing your due diligence on.
2. Make a list of questions. This list will evolve as you learn more about the company. Start with the list given above or make your own based on what you need to know in order to get a full picture of what this company does and what working there would be like.
3. Do desk research. Desk research is the initial research that you do before you begin actively contacting people. This involves online searches, reviewing media coverage, and anything else you can find out from home in a few easy steps. Compile all this research into one document or folder to synthesize what you've learned.
4. Find a middle manager or ex-employees to reach out to. Tell them you are doing some background research on the company and ask them if they wouldn't mind speaking with you for twenty minutes on the phone.

WHAT'S NEXT?

→ E-mail someone you don't know from the company (115)
→ Identify your future boss (130)
→ Map a network in order to find a warm introduction to the company or your future boss (105)
→ Add people from your course pack to your list of people whose careers you admire (108)

LEARN OUTSIDE OF SCHOOL

NONLINEAR CAREERS DEMAND alternative ways of learning. This exercise is not meant to knock school itself. It's an opportunity to take control of your own growth to find a different way to tackle some of the items on your to-learn list (72). Even the most esoteric ways of learning strengthen your ability to hold a question and move yourself forward along your path.

Taking courses outside of school is especially useful when you are still unsure of whether a particular line of inquiry is going to lead toward the next step in your career. You may just want to test it out, build some mission alignment, or bulk up your practical skills.

Taking a course outside of school can also introduce you to a whole new community with different norms, methods of making money, ways of working together, and topics of discussion. Learning opportunities provide a doorway to new communities because they take work. Only people who are really committed actually follow through, and those who are committed stand out from those who just want membership for quick career gains. It is hard to fake work—so the relationships you will build, the insights you will gain, and the skills you will develop will be well deserved and serve you over the whole course of your career regardless of what specific outcome the course has.

A desire to get involved in a community can be its own form of learning and can double your chances of finding new opportunities.

The School for Poetic Computation is a great example of an alternative school that has mastered the relationship between learning and doing. In the summer of 2016, I took a short course called Code Subversions. The description of the course reads as follows:

> *Instead of coding from scratch, we will be remixing, modding and collaging existing technologies to critically explore them. We'll learn about the physical infrastructure of the internet, underlying logic of programming languages and the code behind popular corporate web platforms. We will then use this knowledge to create playful projects that subvert the computational systems we use every day.*

I honestly didn't understand what it meant, but I was intrigued. I spent time on the website going through the profiles of the teachers and past students. It seemed as if it was fluid—no real separation between the teacher and the student at all. It was a community of artists, technologists, philosophers, and academics coming together to challenge what it meant to build and create in the digital age (or at least that was what I thought going in).

When I showed up for the first day of class, it was as if I was transported back ten years to when I was in college. I found a diverse group of people from different walks of life—programmers who had been in the same job for twenty-five years, students just finishing their MFA program, and a Zen chaplain in training who worked at a Buddhist hospice. Everyone had come for their own reasons, and yet we were here to teach and learn together.

The course was difficult and although some of it went over my head I learned a new way of thinking about how technology relates to the world we live in. The intensity worked. In two weeks' worth of two-hour-a-night sessions I became part of a new community and a new world.

From the SFPC community, I discovered an alternative art school fair, and it was there that I met my people. A learning opportunity had led me to find another community that even more closely resembled the life I was building. I met people who had started alternative libraries around the world. They were not explicitly in the art world, nor in the academic world, nor were they library scientists, but somewhere in between. They were practitioners, writers, and book people who understood what I was doing—they were a new group of friends.

The course itself had given me the framework and the permission to continue the journey, which eventually led me to find library people who understood me. Within one day of meeting them I understood my goals for the Sorted Library, my independent library project, simply through hearing their explanations of their work.

Taking a course isn't just about the material you learn. The insights you gain and the people you meet can have unexpected outcomes that are even more important than any original idea you may have thought you were going for.

Each world has its own types of alternative educational paths—apprenticeships in the art world, master classes in the dance and music worlds, journeyman positions in the trades, thirty-day online boot camps in the start-up world, or even alternative art schools in the library world. There are courses, institutions, workshops, and places to learn where people are eager to teach and are looking for someone like you.

THE EXERCISE

To find a course outside of the formal education system, try the following:

1. Consult your list of twenty people who are interesting (99), or your mentor list (148), and look through their information for communities that could lead you to learning opportunities.

2. Consult your to-learn list (72) and brainstorm where you could learn these skills.
3. Browse online and offline school listings and meet-ups for alternative learning communities.

Sign up and go in with an open mind. Embrace the unknown.

WHAT'S NEXT?

→ Update your LinkedIn profile with any new learning programs you've attended or people you've met (17)
→ Go on a solo trip and learn by turning inward (40)
→ E-mail someone you don't know who is connected to what you've just learned (115)

TAKE BETTER NOTES

CLEAR NOTES LEAD to clear thinking. The stream of incoming information is constant and the flow of information will only increase if you tackle the exercises within this book with sincerity. The earlier you build a system for capturing your notes the better, but anytime is a good time to start.

Without developing a clear way of making sense of all this information, important details will be missed, lines of inquiry will be forgotten, and an event recommendation or resource may slip by, stealing away your opportunity to meet new people or learn about an industry.

Recording the small thoughts makes all the difference. The seemingly unimportant, cast-off comments that don't strike you as important to your job search could be the ones that land you your next job. As you may also find when you record and transcribe a stressful situation (152), what you think is happening in the moment may often not correlate at all with the objective reality when viewed later. Good notes are a hedge against this very thing.

These are not the notes you were taught to take in school. They are not an expository recitation of detail. Unlike a straight transcript, they are not meant to capture everything you do or see or read. They are instead a subjective recording of quotes, snippets, insights, full journal entries, or small diagrams that help you explain what you've learned.

Each time you take a note you are taking action on an idea. Simply recording the idea can sometimes be enough to satisfy an inquiry. The good ideas—the good lines of inquiry—will be the ones that you keep pursuing, that generate their own momentum.

I interviewed a soldier in the Canadian military years ago and he told me a line that was ingrained in him during his basic training. He explained that in stressful high-risk situations, "you don't rise to the occasion and become a hero, you fall back to routine and your training." I think about this sentiment all the time. When the perfect idea or job comes along, we won't all of a sudden change our habits, capture it, and take action unless that is what we do every day in our notebooks, with important and unimportant ideas alike.

One of the best note takers I have ever met is a man named Mathias Jakobsen. He created a note-taking system that he calls Think Clearly (www .thnkclrly.com), and he has a whole curriculum that is worth exploring.

THE EXERCISE

These are some of the basics of Mathias's system that have helped me take better notes, along with a few insights from Mathias on their importance. Remember to find the way that works for you.

- **Draw an edge around the page.**
  Take a black pen and before you add anything to your blank page draw an outline around the edge. This will slow you down and center the information. It creates a short ritual that lowers the intimidation of a blank white page and can act as a reminder to be fully present and listen and learn.

- **Give each idea room to breathe.**
  Give an idea a whole page. You may have been trained during

school to take notes one after another until the page was filled. Breaking this habit enables you to see, remember, and process important ideas more clearly. Leaving space around an idea can also signal to you later that there is room to expand, an opportunity to build more ideas. Note taking is suddenly transformed from a process of capturing to an act of creating.

- **Consider hierarchy.**

 Mathias explains that in your mind, your thoughts all have the same importance—there may be patterns and repetition, but a thought is a thought. Putting them to paper is your opportunity to create order and hierarchy. Come up with at least a three-part hierarchy: title; subtitle; bullet point. You may want to underline titles or BLOCK CAP subtitles. Regardless of what you choose, remain consistent. This simple practice made the single biggest difference in how useful my notes have become to me.

- **Draw icons.**

 Drawings help you understand and remember subject matter. They also slow down the process of understanding by forcing you to break abstract concepts down into something tangible. A simple stick figure or icon can lighten the mood and introduce a sense of play to your pages.

- **Create a system and stick to it.**

 Sticking to a single process will give you clarity. Your system can be as simple as the type of notebook you use or the color of your pen. Consistency creates a quick way to compare notes over time, identify trends, and navigate through your journals easily.

The link between the details of note taking and getting a job may not seem obvious, but there is, in fact, a valid correlation. The way that you capture information changes what you pay attention to, what you remember, and what you take action on. It is this change that can be the key that unlocks your next job. It will help bring to the surface new skills to add to your to-learn list (72), as well as other things like insights you've gained from a past mentor. It will help you get the most out of all the work that you are doing as you navigate these fifty ways.

WHAT'S NEXT?

→ Continue getting organized and create a job search spreadsheet (170)
→ Change the way you make decisions (205)
→ Follow up on a question in your notebook by going on a research trip (75)

LOOK FOR ANSWERS IN UNLIKELY PLACES

ANSWERS ARRIVE FROM UNEXPECTED PLACES when you allow yourself to hold a question for an extended period. It involves seeking an answer in different venues, using multiple methods, and approaching problems in unexpected ways. It involves a diligent type of work, such as going back to source material or visiting a physical location directly.

Looking for answers in places you least expect will lead you to meet people you wouldn't otherwise have met. It leads to questions you may not have considered, and as a result, to jobs and careers that may have been hiding in plain sight. This exercise teaches this approach. It's a chance for you to experience a way of being that lies counter to the traditional linear path many follow.

It may seem risky on the surface, but believe me when I tell you that it is useful and that it *will* help you find your next step. This is a hard tactic to try first. If you feel like you need a job tomorrow and are stressed about how you are going to pay your rent in two weeks' time, jump to (143 or 191) and come back to this later.

If you are willing to explore, take a risk, or try something new, this exercise is for you.

In her book *Learning to Walk in the Dark*, Barbara Brown Taylor sets out with the question "How do you walk in the dark?" The way she proceeds to answer it is a great example of holding a question over time. Throughout the book she embarks on a whole range of activities—from a close reading of the Bible to looking at what happens in the darkness (surprisingly positive things) to moving chickens at night when they are calm to going caving to walking under only the moonlight. By letting a single question permeate the experiences of our lives, we will eventually reveal an answer; or at the very least it will be a valuable part of the process.

We don't have to be writers, artists, or academics to have a question and to seek the answer in an unlikely place. Our careers can be avenues for inquiry. They already are a way to learn and to listen to our own lives, but they can also be a path to answering any question that holds us.

We don't always get our dream job right away, in very much the same way as don't always find the answer we are looking for when we set out to find it, but we do get closer. We learn along the way, and we find new questions that can point us in new directions.

THE EXERCISE

1. Choose a length of time you want to hold a question. Setting a time frame for this exercise will give you a rough framework to work within so that you feel a sense of progress as you move through it. You can choose any length of time as long as it is a minimum of one week.
2. For a few weeks before you begin, take note of every question that comes into your head. Write them all down. After some time recording these questions, read them out loud and choose the one that excites you the most.
3. Make a list of all the ways you could explore this question. Think laterally and be as creative as possible. Include the places where you think you are most likely to find an answer as well as the places you

think would be unlikely. Visit both. Try to come up with at least ten different ways to explore the question at hand.

4. Over the course of your time window do at least three of the explorations you've listed. Take notes and record your thoughts as you do so. In addition to these three explorations, look for answers to your question in your everyday life.

5. With these insights in hand, ask yourself what jobs, careers, or contracts you could pursue that would help you deepen your understanding of the question. Add any companies that may fit to your company list (119) or any new skills you would need to learn in order to get such a job to your to-learn list (72).

INQUIRY AT WORK

One of the most unlikely places we may think of looking for an answer is at the job that we are looking to leave. Jobs can be fertile ground for answering a line of inquiry. Choose one question that you identified from the exercises above or a question related to your job search, such as: What are my skills (69)? What do I want to learn next (72)? Or, What path do I want to walk (31)? Try to find the answer to this one question over the duration of one week at your current job. By seeking an answer in our daily grind we start to actively find new meaning in our old routine. It is one layer of thinking overlaid on a life we are already living.

If you find an answer, write it down, but continue to ask the question. Questions can have multiple answers. After the week comes to a close, set aside thirty minutes to consider your answer or answers and how you found them.

WHAT'S NEXT?

→ Discover ways to prove you are mission-aligned (194)
→ Create a course pack to capture all the new information you are discovering (108)
→ Reassess your financial runway to find out how long your money will last (12)

FIELD NOTE: FINDING
INTEREST IN THE DETAILS

EVEN THE MOST BORING PARTS of the job search can be filled with meaning if we know how to pay attention. It is in the moments that others may see as a sidetrack, such as honing a skill, building our mission, or making extra cash from a side job, that we need to remind ourselves to notice the details.

How we deal with these moments is a strong predictor of whether we can stay the course and take the long-arc approach to getting a job and building a career that is perfect for us. Practicing this skill strengthens our ability to delay gratification in the name of the longer vision of our careers. How do you practically remain engaged and find meaning in even the dullest of situations?

I started working at a part-time job and one thing I disliked about it was the commute. Three days a week I would wake up to the alarm and crowd onto a busy train platform and wait for a packed train to a bustling city center with people all trying to do the same thing.

After a month of making this commute, I began to realize that my mood and the first several hours of my day were affected by my ride. In some ways the city reflected back to me what I felt, and during the course of the subway ride that feeling would become magnified. If I was happy, I saw happiness and the sun reflecting off the cityscape. If I woke up feeling upset, the commute amplified the feeling, delivering me to work in a harried state.

I decided that I wanted to take control of my commute and my feelings. Initially, I tried just noticing one thing a day and writing about it on my phone, like how the pattern on a woman's dress matched that of the advertisement behind her. Within a week I was bored. It felt random and meaningless, only exacerbating my arbitrary positive or negative feelings.

At the time I was doing research about the power of constraints to breed creativity. The French group of intellectuals knows as the Oulipo were a group of writers, artists, and mathematicians who championed this type of thinking. I decided that I would apply their idea of constraints to my commute—to try to wrestle back my emotional state from whatever I saw on the subway, to find some point of interest.

So I gave myself constraints. Each day I would stand on the platform between two tracks in a small, one-hundred-square-foot space between an elevator shaft and the backside of a staircase. I would return to this same space every day. I decided that I would try to record everything in this space.

I began taking notes.

SOUTH WALL

There are 130 white tiles on the south wall in the space. There is one door. The tiles can be understood in the following way from top to bottom: [(Row of 9) × 4] + [(Row of 6 + Row of 5) × 8] + Row of 6 The rows of 6 include a small sliver of a tile 1-inch wide on the left side of the door. The whole wall alternates between 3-inch vertical and 6-inch vertical tile.

THE DOOR

The door leads to a room that occupies the space beneath the stairs that lead down to the platform. The room is labeled "STA SCRUBBER ROOM 212-712-4236." The sign that states this is above the door, posted on the 2.5-inch door frame. It is a

black sign with white text. The sign's bottom edge was accidentally painted, eras-
ing the majority of the black border along the lower edge. It looks to be a result of a
hasty paint job with no taping.

As I became more familiar with this space I began to care about it. I knew where the maintenance worker who'd installed the metal grille did a rushed job and missed a screw. I began to notice how long things were left in the space, such as the note that was left written on the wall and answered two days later by another stranger. I noticed subtleties. Over the course of six months I became the uncontested world's expert on this hundred-square-foot portion of the DeKalb platform.

My commute shifted. I was engaged. I looked forward to finding out what had happened in the days before. On the subway itself, I was busy recollecting any other small details I could remember from my time in the space that day and the next day I would clarify them. My three- to eight-minute wait each day several times a week had resulted in a lengthy body of work. More than thirty pages of details and a journal of every item taken out and left in the space.

One morning I checked my mail as I walked to the platform. A friend had sent a postcard from Bali—she described the colorful visual of the markets and rice fields of the town where she was and she finished with the line "Belief brings peace here—observing as well."

I couldn't have agreed more. I had found that same level of peace, of grounding, of engagement in objectively the most boring transitory space I passed through each day. It was filled with meaning in the details. This is the same muscle we can bring to any moment that we encounter— especially moments of a job search that are tedious or boring.

Noticing the details will help you get unstuck. Finding meaning in the details, with discipline, over a prolonged period of time produces a type of purpose that can help you carry on. Even the best job search will still have boring and routine activities, and by finding interest in the details you strengthen your ability to take on this work and delay that anxiety-producing need for immediacy.

NETWORKING

LIST TWENTY PEOPLE WHOSE CAREERS YOU ADMIRE

THIS IS A LIST you will continue to add to and use consistently whether you are searching for a job or not. It is a practice akin to creating a course pack (108)—it will provide inspiration, direction, and unexpected opportunities.

This is not about listing celebrities. The less famous someone is, the better the fit for this list. This is about creating a list of people who are one, five, or ten steps ahead of you in pursuit of your dream career. You don't need to know them. You may only be drawn to a single aspect of their career. In fact, it can be better sometimes if you not know them— the myth of what they do, how they have navigated their nonlinear career, can provide all the motivation you need to take the next step in the right direction.

These people will become potential allies, the people to track and watch out for at events. They will be future bosses, peers, and motivational beacons that will help you as you follow your path. Challenge yourself to seek out and follow the online trail of people you've read an interesting article about or heard mentioned in a conversation. Look them up later, read their bio, view the work they have done, and see who they are connected to (105).

Make it easy for yourself to capture names on the go—whatever system you decide to use, if it's a notebook, a folder on your computer, or a simple spreadsheet, consider and think about the one that works best for you. The easier you make the process of capturing the information, the more likely you are to do it.

Once you have your list of interesting people, it's time to dig a little deeper. Follow these people on social media, sign up for their e-mails, and do some research to figure out where they are speaking or where they hang out. It doesn't matter if you actually meet them or not. These are the places where you will find and meet others who are one step ahead or one step behind you in their careers: these are perfect peers to have in your nonlinear journey.

As you review profiles and portfolios and take note of the institutions, conferences, media, and programs or companies that are mentioned, consider these as valuable leads that may resurface or that you should add to your company list (119) or your to-learn list (72).

Jobs have come from less likely places.

THE EXERCISE

1. Make a list of the twenty people whose careers you admire. If no one comes to mind start researching the mavericks in any given field. They are often known by the people in the industry, speak at the industry conferences, and are often talked about within industry circles.
2. Seek out the people behind those who you look up to most. If you have a number of people on high pedestals, in the public spotlight, or who are busy entrepreneurs, do some digging to find out who they work with. Who are the people on the wings, supporting these superstars or managing their businesses?
3. Browse the various "top 30," "top 50," and "top 100" lists for the most creative, innovative, and successful people out there. The Forbes 30 Under 30 list alone includes more than six hundred peo-

ple annually, so start there if you are stuck for ideas. You will have your work cut out for you. Be judicious with the people you choose from these lists. Visit their individual websites, read their work, see who they are connected to and who they reference; add these people to your list as well. Take these lists with a healthy sense of humility. I recommend starting with lists that are two or three years old. It forces you to see that most of these people will have changed jobs, changed companies, or moved on to new exciting work. This will give you a sense of the cyclicity of these listings and a gentle reminder that we all have ups and downs regardless of how much or how little publicity we get.

4. Make a note of the events and conferences that you are most drawn to and see if you can get ahold of speaker and attendee lists. Browse the speaker lists from previous years as well.

5. Research every individual on your list. Follow them on social media and make note of any events they speak at or attend.

WHAT'S NEXT?

→ E-mail someone from the above list that you don't know (115)

→ Choose one person and interview him or her (34)

→ Take a look at where and what the people on your list studied. Take a course outside of school (82) or add a new skill to your to-learn list (72)

→ Identify a mentor who is a few years ahead of you and reach out (148)

HELP FIVE PEOPLE

THE DALAI LAMA coined the term "wise selfishness" to refer to the act of helping others. Inherent in that phrase is the interconnectedness of all things—helping others enables us to detangle our thoughts, gain perspective, and build momentum, by grounding us in what we have to offer. In effect, helping another is actually helping oneself.

Helping people is a practice and an alternative to the old-school networking that we are often told to do. It will help you get a job because it changes the way you meet and interact with people without any of the anxiety of trading favors at networking events. Helping people doesn't need to consist of grand gestures or traveling to foreign countries. Helping someone starts with the little, simple acts of kindness—listening and empathizing with a friend, going to an event a little bit early to help set something up, or offering the right word of encouragement at the right time. Good help is predicated on paying attention to others and to practicing a deeper type of listening than we are used to.

The practice of deep listening is grounded in a line of poetry by Hafiz, the great fourteenth-century Persian poet, which asks you to listen to people as if you were listening to the last words of your dying master.

Spending several weeks with this idea, coupled with the practice I learned through the Rockwood Leadership Institute, highlighted just how little I had listened prior. Try it. Listen to everyone today as if the words they speak were the last words of your revered mentor. Speed and efficiency cajole us into guessing where a sentence is going and re-sponding before the person even finishes the thought.

If we do stop and listen we pick up on ways to help. We start to no-tice people wanting us to ask about things we would have missed. This is not an exercise you can fast-track. It will feel inauthentic if you do. You have to lead with listening. To truly experience wise selfishness you have to set out not to help people but simply to listen.

This is a paradigm shift and a different approach from the archetype of the cartoonish ego-led networker—doing favors in exchange for ones in return. Listening with an ear to help doesn't involve trading favors—it requires presence.

Listen and notice what people are asking for, what they want you to ask about, and what they need but may not be comfortable saying until you invite them to share. Help people with these quiet requests. Help them answer these questions. You are listening to understand needs; and then, like an endurance athlete, it is about the long race, maintaining the memory of your conversation and holding it as you walk through your life just in case you happen upon the right resource, the right book, the right person, the right phrase, which you can then share back.

You can't rush this. It is a way of being, not a task to complete.

A direct "What can I do to help you?" can be a hard question to an-swer. People are often embarrassed to ask for help or unsure of what you have in mind in the way of support. But if you listen and ask another layer of questions, you will start to see the world as a memory game—and your job is simply to remember where the tiles are and wait to make the right match.

THE EXERCISE

1. Don't expect anything. Although wise selfishness is rooted in the idea that we are all connected and that helping others is also an act of helping oneself, hold no expectations that the person you're helping will help you in return.

2. Spend two weeks treating everyone's words as if they were the last words of your master. Give them reverence. Ask follow-up questions and listen for what they are expressing a need for. There is no need to announce your support, just hold their needs in your mind and see if you can find the perfect way to help them over the course of the coming weeks.

3. If you are feeling inspired, review your course pack (108) and see if there are any articles or resources that would be worth sending to the people you have had the opportunity to listen to over the last two weeks.

4. When you come across a great resource for one of these people, send a note right away. It can be a quick text, a three-line e-mail, or a note in the mail. Don't overthink it. Immediacy should trump perfection. Be aware of what you are committing to (59). "Help" doesn't need to come in the form of big, time-consuming commitments. Remember that simply listening and asking the right questions can often be enough.

WHAT'S NEXT?

→ Decide when to work for free (197)
→ Renegotiate any outstanding commitments that remain perpetually on your to-do list (59)
→ Try on a new way of being while helping others (43)

MAP A NETWORK

MANY EFFECTIVE JOB-HUNTING METHODS rely on the ability to find and contact the right person without being socially awkward or imposing. The techniques below will help you map a network—the first step before reaching out to people you don't yet know.

Our network of relationships form the basis for how we understand and process information. For example we rely on our networks to determine the validity of the advice we get—we trust one friend when it comes to career advice and another for restaurant recommendations. This way of understanding is based on a complex and always shifting network map that operates unseen in the background.

A few years ago there were two moments that showed the ultimate network map of the world: the Madoff scandal and the Ice Bucket Challenge. During the aftermath coverage of the Madoff scandal, for a short moment news networks were focused on revealing all of the connections and relationships between the elite in America, detailing how they had all invested with Bernie Madoff. Money had moved based on trust and on relationships and for a moment that web of relationships was visible. A similar thing happened during the height of the Ice Bucket Challenge as individuals who accepted the challenge nominated other people they were close to and if you paid attention you could track the relationships expanding ever outward, all while millions of dollars were being raised for an important cause.

In one example, Bernie Madoff stole millions of dollars, and in the other millions were raised for ALS.

These two examples showcase the power and reality of how money moves across a network map. Job opportunities move in similar ways. The simple act of considering and mapping a network isn't good or bad. It is what we do with those relationships and friends that matters. This exercise is a chance for you to make visible the often invisible networks that we navigate every day.

THE EXERCISE

This exercise will create the foundation for other exercises in the book, such as finding your future boss (130), talking to a mentor you don't yet know (115), and compiling your list of twenty people (99). Follow these simple steps to map a network around a person.

1. Choose a person you want to meet. Don't have someone in mind? Choose from your list of twenty people (99) or consult the chapter on finding your future boss (130).
2. Search for this person through LinkedIn, Instagram, or Facebook and see if you can identify any friends of theirs who are equally intriguing.
3. Keep notice of any mutual friends but if you can't find any direct connections, identify people who seem close to them and follow the same process for these people.
4. Continue until you have an expansive network map based on online profiles, Instagram tags, and Facebook friend searches of the person you began with.
5. Choose one person from this network map. Don't worry if you don't know anyone on the map—choose the person who seems the

most interesting and accessible to you. Send the person an e-mail using the template found in the chapter on e-mailing someone you don't know (115). If you can't find the person's e-mail address, try guessing by searching for other employees in the same company and figuring out the corporate e-mail address format.

WHAT'S NEXT?

→ Identify a person from your mapping exercise who can be either a future boss (130) or on your list of twenty people (99)
→ Reflect on your dream job and its relationship to the network that you've mapped (31)
→ Prepare your personal story for an interview (191)
→ Help five people (102)

CREATE A COURSE PACK

WE CONSUME SO MUCH MEDIA TODAY. Articles fly by. Images scroll up and disappear. We read headlines and we forget them. The information can easily overwhelm us. Hours can slip by and we don't even realize the choice we've made to spend our time in front of our computer or on our phone.

Beginning in the sixteenth century, people began to create commonplace books. These were personal collections of quotes, small ideas, phrases, and the ephemera of everyday life that they would want to learn from and keep handy. It was different from a journal—it was a scrapbook of interests. It was the old-fashioned version of what I call a "course pack."

While things are much different today from how they were several hundred years ago, a course pack can still offer a valuable method of slowing down. Your course pack will allow you to pull bits and pieces out of the fast-paced river of information and make sense of it during slower moments. It will help you learn more about yourself and help you uncover patterns in your own tastes that you would have never noticed.

The practice of creating a course pack can also help you strengthen belief in your own nonlinear path.

I started my practice of keeping a course pack by accident more than ten years ago. I cut out articles from magazines that I found interesting or that inspired me in some way. I was just throwing all these articles and profiles and pictures into a drawer. Eventually, I realized I needed to reclaim the drawer for other things, so I decided to photocopy all the pieces of paper and ephemera I had collected. It ended up being more than three hundred pages, and while I was at the copy shop I had it bound so that a whole drawer of information could fit neatly on my shelf.

The practice stuck and worked in ways that I wouldn't have initially imagined. I began to remember people from articles I'd clipped five years before. By memorializing these articles and reminding myself of them whenever I flipped through the book, I made myself remember the people who I thought were interesting and who I would have otherwise forgotten, as they generally had very little notoriety or fame.

Every now and then I'd notice someone out in the world whom I'd collected in my course pack. I'd worry about introducing myself, not wanting to seem too forward or creepy by saying I recognized them from something I'd read ages ago. But I came up with a good solution. Now I introduce myself and tell them right away that I have a really good memory, almost photographic, and I read about them in an article several years ago and just wanted to say hello. People are flattered. They usually comment that they wish they had a memory like that, and the conversation continues.

Some of the people I have approached this way have become my best friends and trusted colleagues. You don't need a good memory—but you do need a good process for remembering.

The system you create to capture information that inspires you needs to be simple. Make your own system. Be wary of adapting an app or someone else's system without first asking yourself if there is an easier way that more directly serves your own needs. A system can be a simple bookmark folder called "course pack" in your browser, a physical drawer you put articles in, or a tag you add to photos. The more complicated your system is, the harder it is to follow every day. Lower the bar for yourself. Make it as simple as possible, deferring much of the organizing work for a later day when you have time and a sense of excitement to search for patterns.

THE EXERCISE

1. **Identify your sources.**
   Make a list of all the places you are most likely to come across inspiring information, articles, and photos.

2. **Create a simple system.**
   For each of these sources create a method to flag, label, or cut out the pieces of inspiration when you first see them so you are adding as little extra work to your plate as possible.

3. **Organize it when you feel like it.**
   Once a year, organize and collect all the pieces of inspiring information and put them into one format. For example, I like to print, photocopy, and bind the articles, but others prefer doing it digitally.

4. **Browse and look for patterns.**
   When you're bored, demoralized with work, or just looking for some inspiration, flip through your course pack and make notes in it. Leave it on your bookshelf or open on your desktop. Reread your favorite articles, hunt for patterns, and follow up on leads that you find hidden inside. Observe how your thinking and tastes have evolved over time.

WHAT'S NEXT?

→ Review your course pack and add any interesting people to this list (99)
→ Write fiction about yourself, using the articles you selected as inspiration (37)
→ Update your LinkedIn profile as your future self (17)
→ Follow up on a question from your course pack by planning a research trip (75)

RECONNECT WITH FIVE MENTORS FROM YOUR PAST

THIS EXERCISE IS ABOUT building momentum rather than the advice the mentors will share. For this to work, you don't even need to have had formal mentors—it's the informal kind that count. Someone you have turned to in the past or a colleague who gives good advice or simply someone you look up to will do just fine for this exercise. The most important thing is that you have five distinct conversations.

Daniel was twenty-six years old and had been working at the same restaurant in Toronto for six years. In his spare time, he and two friends started a small nonprofit called Dudebox that threw concerts in offbeat venues like parking garages and gyms while raising money for charity. Over three years, they had raised more than $150,000 for various charities. Dudebox was a side project for Daniel that was doing a lot of good.

Dudebox's growth made Daniel decide that he wanted to do something more meaningful with his time during the workday. Like so many of us, he wanted to find a way to bring the sense of purpose he felt after hours into the rest of his life. He needed a new career.

He began meeting anyone he could for coffee and applying to an endless array of jobs. Person after person, coffee after coffee, and application after application, the search led to only one thing: emotional ups and downs. He finally got an interview for a job as executive director of a small nonprofit that he had applied to online. He walked into the windowless office, sat down across from the interviewer, and felt an emptiness. He responded mechanically and sped through the interview quickly, leaving without even remembering what was said. He didn't get the job.

Instead of continuing on as he was, Daniel decided to reach out to five people who had helped him in the past.

The final of the five mentors Daniel reached out to was the person who finally gave him a break. It was an hour into the conversation, and it was looking like the conversation was wrapping up with no big insights or next steps when his mentor suggested offhandedly, "Why don't you get in touch with Manifesto?" Manifesto was one of the organizations that Daniel had been raising money for through Dudebox for years. The people running it were his friends.

Manifesto had always been right there in front of him throughout the six months of job searching, and yet he hadn't thought of getting in touch about a job. He sent a note when he got home and the conversations began. Manifesto was in the middle of an internal transition and the staff were looking to hire someone to coordinate their next festival. They responded right away and asked Daniel to come in and speak with them. They decided to test working together formally with a short-term contract and gave Daniel a chance to prove what he could do, getting paid for what he loved and believed in. Two years later he is still doing it.

Sometimes the value in mentors isn't that they bring new information to the table or that they have some sort of deep expertise in a specific area. The value can be in a single line at the end of an hour-long conversation. Sometimes what it takes is someone else pointing out what's right in front of you. You can be so attached to how you see the pieces of your life fitting together that you would never recognize that one of the relationships you have been building as a result of a side project could actually lead to your next full-time job.

Approaching conversations with mentors without the expectation of sage advice liberates both them and you. You don't need to walk away with a recommendation, a referral, or a job for it to be a success. It is about putting yourself in front of someone who believes in you and seeing what happens.

THE EXERCISE

1. Make a list of five people who have given you advice in the past five years. Don't worry if they are not related to the career move you are making now. The more diverse the group, the better.
2. E-mail each one and schedule a time to chat. Ask them the same questions you are asking yourself now regarding your career, no matter how relevant you think it is to their present experience. These people are already part of your path and your success, if only in a small way, and they will be honored to be asked for advice. If they question why you are asking them, tell them it's because you appreciated advice they previously gave you, even if it didn't end up working out.
3. Listen to everyone, but act only on the advice that resonates with you. You will get a lot of conflicting advice in this exercise. This is part of the process. If you have doubts, ask your friend what he or she thinks during your biweekly call (6).

WHAT'S NEXT?

→ Update your job search spreadsheet, tracking all your potential opportunities and meetings (170)
→ Interview a mentor with the goal of uncovering the uncertainties in his or her career path (34)
→ Ask past mentors what skills they think you have and update your list of skills (69)

E-MAIL SOMEONE
YOU DON'T KNOW

THERE IS A COMMON ADAGE in fund-raising: ask for money and you will get advice, ask for advice and you will get money. This holds true for the job search as well. Asking for advice is one of the most powerful ways to learn while moving forward along your career trajectory.

Asking for advice from someone you don't know can be intimidating. One way to get over the intimidation is to be informed. Do enough research that you begin to see yourself as working on the same side of the table—a peer instead of simply a student looking to get free information.

This shift can be a high bar and could even feel paralyzing, but it doesn't have to. The majority of people do little to no preparation when they e-mail someone asking for advice. There is a simple rule you should follow that will ensure you are never this person—for every minute you ask of someone, put two times that amount into preparation. Ask for thirty minutes, spend sixty minutes preparing.

The power in doing this extra work extends beyond common courtesy and even beyond a more informed eventual discussion. The power is in the preparation itself. Through my prediscussion research, I typically uncover interesting resources, new people I have never heard about, companies I become excited about, and worlds I want to become a part of. By the time I sit down to e-mail the individual I already feel thankful to him or her, without the person having said a word to me. Before you send this e-mail, release yourself of expectations by deciding you don't need anything from this person and that the insight you have gained from your research is already enough.

If you blind e-mail multiple people with the same request for career advice, you miss out on the opportunity to stumble onto your future boss (130) or the next company you are going to work for (119). You are in control of what you learn. You have the opportunity to learn directly from people who are living this information.

The people you choose determine the excitement you are going to feel when you do this exercise. If this feels like a dull process, you may not have chosen the right person. Go back to either your network map (105) or your course pack (108) and find new people you are actually excited to learn about, hear from, and talk to. The choice is yours.

THE EXERCISE

Part 1: The Research

Here is what you should spend sixty minutes learning before you e-mail people you don't know.

1. **Follow their online trail.**
   Read their publications and articles and immerse yourself in the projects that they share on their personal websites. Connect with and learn about the people they collaborate with or have worked with in the past. Follow the trail as far as you can.

2. **Understand their timeline.**
   You shouldn't have to ask them to tell you their employment or project history if you show up prepared. They will be more likely

to engage with you when you reach out if you have done your work. This career history is generally available online or on people's LinkedIn pages.

3. **What questions does their work address?**
   If their work doesn't directly address a consistent question, what question or need does their company provide an answer for?

4. **Be able to answer the question "What do you think I work on?"**
   Know what question their work is trying to answer and how they have been attempting to answer it. Know the industry, their approach, and as much about their recent projects as possible.

5. **Why them? Why now?**
   Have a good answer for why you chose to reach out to them specifically and why you did that now. The more specific and authentic this reason is, the better the response will be.

Part 2: The E-mail

Armed with this information, you are now ready to reach out and ask for an opportunity to speak with your new potential adviser. Your e-mail should be informed by the work that you've done and information that you've learned in preparation for sending it.

Here is a framework for an e-mail that you can adapt and make your own. The total e-mail should be no more than five sentences long.

1. **The Setup**
   Tell them why you respect them, why you think their career path is interesting, and why their advice is important to you.

2. **The Request**
   Ask for thirty minutes of their time to meet in person and get their advice on:

a. A question you are asking that relates to an issue you saw them address in your research; or

b. Something tangible (a specific career decision you have to make)

WHAT'S NEXT?

→ Record any commitments you make during or after the meeting in your commitment book (59)

→ If you didn't get the response you desired, use the techniques discussed for how to win over someone who cast you aside (155)

→ Prepare your personal story so it is interview-ready (191)

MAKE A COMPANY LIST

FOR THIS EXERCISE, let go of any preconceived ideas of where you should work. You will need to think laterally. If you don't make an attempt at a creative and exhaustive list, you will be left with the five companies you have known about for years or those suggested to you by others, and you instantly lower your chances of finding something new.

When you begin talking to people, friends, and mentors, they will often suggest companies that you should join. These suggestions generally fall into two different categories: companies tied to what you love and companies based on the last one you worked at.

No doubt you have a friend who, upon learning you are looking for a job, asks right away, "Well, what are you passionate about?" Your friend may even suggest that you seemed excited when you were talking about your recent trip and maybe you should consider working at a travel company. Even if you love traveling and you were excited about your trip, there is a good chance that retelling happy stories from a time away is not a good indication of a future career direction or a company to add to your list.

If you are like most of us and you aren't really sure what you are passionate about or what companies typify this—don't worry about it. Ignore this friend's advice. There are multiple ways to find companies to work for without knowing what your passion is. Passion is something we build through work and inquiry, both of which are great ways to identify companies.

If you build a company list by asking yourself only what you liked or didn't like at your last job, you will often end up moving across the aisle, for example, from a consultant role to becoming the client or maybe from a grantee to a funder. A related but different experience.

The goal of this exercise should be to uncover new companies that you may have never considered—companies that you had never envisioned working for and yet that you arrive at with a clear sense of everyday purpose and an answer to the important question, "What are you doing right now?" (182, Everyday Purpose box)

Here are a few ideas to get you started. Make lists of companies:

Based on what you want to learn next (72)
That work at the intersection of two industries you are interested in
Based on a question you want to pursue (133)
Based on your personal sense of gravity (27)
That your just-ahead mentor would have considered (148)

This list should be filled with new companies you have never considered before. Don't forget about all the opportunities and businesses that could be stepping-stones to that ideal job. We often miss seeing the opportunities on the path, focusing only on those at the summit.

THE EXERCISE

1. Start your list with five dream companies you want to work for.
2. Consult your to-learn list (72) and add companies where you would be able to learn some of these skills.
3. Add an additional five companies to your company list by considering the ideas listed above.
4. Prioritize your list based on what you want to learn most.

WHAT'S NEXT?

→ Create a company brief for a company on your list (78)
→ Find a job title that resonates with you (176)
→ Identify your future boss at a company on your list (130)
→ Send this e-mail to the company you want to work for (184)

CHOOSE THREE EVENTS
TO ATTEND

You don't have to meet everyone in the room. You don't need to rush the speaker or make sure people never forget you in order to get a job. Going to events doesn't need to be the domain of the extrovert. There are other benefits to attending an event that you'll notice once you release yourself from the expectation that you need to "work the room" and leave with endless lunch and coffee meetings set up. You don't have to go too far out of your comfort zone to find value in attending events. For example, you can use the experience to:

Familiarize yourself with the language of a new industry (43)
Help demonstrate that you are committed to the mission of a company (194)
Answer a line of inquiry that you may have (133)
Practice introducing yourself in a new way (126)
Search for an answer in an unlikely place (90)

You get to choose what the event means to you regardless of how it's billed. An event meant to give emerging professionals a chance to meet each other can be something you passively watch from the sideline. You can skip the panels and just attend lunch. You decide what you want out of it—rename the event for this new purpose in your head and take a friend to your version.

Years ago, I interviewed a professional poker player who had won the World Series of Poker, and he told me one key to winning is to bet consistently on the hands that are 60–65 percent in your favor. He began explaining the difference between an outcome and a decision. "Most people don't realize," he said, "you can have a bad outcome and a great decision." Any bet that you make where you have a 65 percent chance or greater of winning is a good decision regardless of the outcome—you just have to stay consistent. When you confuse a bad outcome with a bad decision you emotionally react and you change how you play, often waiting for the perfect hand, which rarely comes and can't be predicted.

This theory can apply to almost any situation when you want to take a calculated and nonemotional approach.

When I first moved to New York City, I would force myself to go to all the book readings, cultural events, and social enterprise events I could find. Sometimes I would travel for forty-five minutes only to realize that the event had been canceled without notice. In these moments I would question what I was doing at this random loft in a neighborhood I didn't know, and then I would always turn back to the poker advice—bad outcome, good decision. It always served as just enough reinforcement to keep on going to events even when I didn't feel like it. I was making good decisions, giving myself the chance to meet people at companies I could work for, fellow writers I could share stories with, and a community of support that seven years later has given me some of my closest friends.

When I attended dozens of youth conferences each year, I would find myself sitting in endless panels and hearing various keynote speeches. I developed a method of taking notes where I would write down the questions that came into my head. Some of them would be related to what the person on stage was saying and others would be based on whatever I had done that day or was reading at the time. The speeches served as a backdrop, and I gave myself permission to fade in and out; what I was most engaged in was my own thoughts. It was a way to stay interested, to find value for myself regardless of what I was supposed to be doing. Sometimes the best events were the ones where I met no one new but wrote down a question or company in my notebook to research. These small personal moments led to new perspectives, and in unexpected ways they ended up leading me to job opportunities long after I had left the events that sparked them.

THE EXERCISE

Here are three points—originally from my first book, *Making Good*—that will help you select which events to go to and approach them in a stress-free, grounded way.

1. **Don't bet on only one.**
   There might be one event you've heard great things about that includes everyone you need to meet with incredible access. However, if going to this event means that you have to spend all your resources for the year, don't do it. The key to meeting the right people is to attend as many events as possible rather than going to "the perfect one."

2. **Expect to fail.**
   When a venture capitalist invests in ten companies, he or she expects to lose the money on half of the investments, break even on two, make a modest sum on one or two, and hopefully have one or two runaway successes. Apply this principle to all the events you attend. By doing so, you will expect less from each event, be more relaxed, build real relationships, and eventually find that one opportunity you are looking for.

3. **Pay more and play less.**
   If you are going to events every night and you still aren't meeting the right people, then it is time to pay a little more (be it in energy,

time, or money) and play a little less. A good way to do this is to add up all the money and time you are prepared to commit and then divide it between six or eight events. Aim to spend all your resources that year on only those events. Paying a little more for one or a little less for another enables you to find that elusive balance, no matter how you divide it up.

WHAT'S NEXT?

→ Commit to doing these four things if you are feeling overwhelmed (47)
→ Find a friend in the same situation (6)
→ Identify three things that you can do to build your mission alignment (194)

PRACTICE DIFFERENT WAYS OF INTRODUCING YOURSELF

THE MOST MUNDANE OF SITUATIONS can be emotional minefields when you are in between jobs. A casual gathering at a friend's house can turn south as soon as someone asks, "What do you do?"

Most people who ask this seemingly innocuous question are only marginally paying attention to your answer, and most are looking to pick out something you say that they can ask a "smart" next question about. What you say determines what their follow-up question is. It also determines how they perceive you.

The stakes in social situations can feel artificially high. The idea that we should always be networking is pervasive and can lead to feeling like we should be meeting more people instead of being present in the conversations we are in.

The truth is, you don't need to have the perfect introduction that will convince everyone you meet that you are the most interesting and employable person in the room. Give it up. There is an easier way, and it isn't nearly as scary or anxiety inducing as you'd think. It is time to try something different.

This exercise is about equipping yourself with several ways to introduce yourself to create a conversation that is exciting and reflective of where you are at this particular moment. Just as we feel differently in different settings and with different people or at different times of the day, this gives you a repertoire of responses that best fit with the circumstances at hand. You get to consciously choose what conversation you want to have and lead the conversation there by way of your introduction of choice.

Now the conversation is in your control. This exercise turns a moment of fear or anxiety into a moment of play.

THE EXERCISE

Here are some of the ways you can introduce yourself. Follow the templates below and write your introduction. Always consider what kind of responses your introduction will elicit and if that is taking you toward or away from the conversation you are hoping to have.

- **If you want to talk about an industry or job function:**

    I work in the _____ industry helping them to [insert the general purpose behind your function].

    Leave the function a little generic so that it gives you more room to maneuver and discover what it is you actually want to do in that area of work. Examples could include working "on the business side," "on the creative side," or "in production." Answering in this generic way widens the potential job descriptions you could have, as well as the conversation. Regardless of the follow-up questions, you can talk more about the industry or go into more detail about what that area of work looks like within a specific industry.

- **If you are interested in multiple potential career paths:**

    Introduce all your potential career paths in one sentence with an introduction like: *I work at the point where ____ meets ____ meets ____.*

    This is one of my favorite introductions. It enables you to include three diverse or unconnected potential careers. By saying you work at an intersection, you get the opportunity to dive into any one of them if people ask you to explain any further. You can even ask them how they see these three things fitting together. This answer creates flexible conversations that can often take a more exploratory turn.

- **If you want to talk about your lunch:**

  Well, today I worked on making the best sandwich I have had in a while. [Explain the sandwich.]

  I include this introduction as an example of how you really can talk about anything when asked about what you do or where you work. Sometimes not talking about what you do explicitly actually enables you to create a real connection that breaks the mold of the normal expectations of an event.

  Politicians and media spokespeople redirect questions all the time toward what they want to talk about. You can do the same. If the person you are talking to asks what you do for a second time, then he or she may actually have real interest. In this case, go ahead and talk about your work; but if you are feeling like talking about something unrelated to work or occupation, most of the time the person you are talking to will be refreshingly grateful to tell you what he or she had for lunch in return.

- **If you want to talk about what you are learning:**

  I am learning how to do _____ right now by [explain how you are learning it].

  People will often then ask why you are learning to do whatever it is, and you can jump into the details of your newly acquired knowledge. You can tell them about learning something from an unexpected place (90), someone you met along the path (72), or what it would mean to apply this new knowledge. This is also a great way to talk about any books you are currently reading.

- **If you want to talk about your hobby:**

  This past month I spent a lot of time working on [name your hobby].

  People are just as interested in what you do in your spare time. We are socialized to lead with questions about work as an ice-breaker. Start talking about your hobby and the conversation will flow—it may even lead you to an unexpected idea about how to turn your hobby into a full-time job.

- **If you want to talk about a choice you have to make:**

  I am working on deciding right now between [describe your two choices].

  In this example, the two choices could be two different career trajectories, two different cities you would like to work in, or two different things you want to learn. The conversation will automatically turn to helping you make that decision and you will receive yet another valuable opinion to factor into your decision-making process (205).

- **If you want to talk about a past project:**

  Well, to give you an idea, a recent project I worked on was [insert description].

  This is a great way to introduce yourself if you have a portfolio career filled with different projects spanning a wide range of topics and types. Choose the project that you think best connects with the person you're talking to, and give a specific example instead of a broad explanation. This will invariably lead into more details, your motivations, and what projects are next for you.

WHAT'S NEXT?

→ Prepare your personal story so it is interview-ready (191)
→ Find a new community while learning something new (82)
→ Learn how to talk to a recruiter (173)

FIND YOUR FUTURE BOSS

A GOOD BOSS can make the job. You may want someone you can learn from who you actively feel partnered with, or maybe you're looking for someone you can laugh with at company events. Either way, judging and finding the right personality in a boss is impossible to do online. It will happen in conversation as you walk your path, while you're learning and asking questions.

It is hard to know if your future boss is a personality fit until you meet him or her, so this exercise is about doing what is in your control—identifying as many of them as possible. These meetings are not just one-sided transactions. A major part of a boss's job is hiring and developing a pool of great talent—the boss needs to meet you too.

THE EXERCISE

This exercise should be done after you have spent some time clarifying your path (31) and when you feel clear about what you want to learn next (72). Choosing who to reach out to is part intuition and part guesswork. This deserves its own set of rules that can help frame how and who you reach out to.

1. **Aim higher than you expect.**

   It is better to be passed down than to be passed over. If your target company has more than sixty employees, find the person you want to work for and go one level up. If your target company has under sixty employees, go for the CEO or whoever runs the particular department you want to work in.

2. **Find that person's contact information.**

   Do the same research in this case that you would for contacting someone you don't know (115). Find the person's e-mail address or test out any informed hunches you come up with via searching online.

3. **Get an introduction.**

   Many of the previous exercises are designed to help you meet more people in your field so that when you are ready to meet your future boss, you now have someone who can make an introduction for you. If you don't have an intro path, try mapping your network (105) or jump right into sending the e-mail that will get you the job (184).

4. **Reverse reference the company**

   This is an important step to take once you are interviewing with the company. See if you can find a few people who have worked in the company and have now moved on. Reach out by saying, "I am doing some referencing and saw that you worked at [this company] during [whatever years] and was wondering if you would have ten minutes to talk with me about [your future boss's name]." These light innocuous e-mails show that you are doing your research and that you take your research seriously. These reference-checking e-mails are some of the only e-mails that are okay to send on

LinkedIn if you can't find an e-mail readily available. Be open and tell this person that you are considering working with his or her previous employer and ask what the team there is like to work with, what motivates the company, and what the internal dynamics within the company are. If you feel comfortable, ask why the person left. People will often be very forthcoming, and you will learn useful information that will help you in your interview.

5. **E-mail your future boss.**
Once you have done your research, send your future boss a variation of the e-mail that will get you the job (184). There is a particular way of framing your skills and your mission that will help your e-mail stand out and get you the next meeting you need to get the job.

WHAT'S NEXT?

→ Send an adapted version of the e-mail that will get you the job to your future boss (184)
→ Learn how to write your own job description (200)
→ Update the list of people whose careers you admire (99)

FIELD NOTE: CULTIVATING CURIOSITY

QUESTIONS ARE AT THE HEART of the job search. There are the questions you ask yourself and those you ask mentors and peers, and then there are the questions you have to ask when the person across the desk turns to you after an interview and says, "So what do you want to know from me?"

It's strange to consider how rarely we actually spend time improving the quality of the questions we ask or thinking about how we ask questions. The questions you ask speak to the kind of person you are. They demonstrate and showcase your knowledge and can separate you from peers during the job search.

A few years ago, I was on vacation and sitting at a bar with a friend in a small restaurant. Next to us was a woman in active clothes, reading her book and eating tapas. Eventually we all struck up a conversation and began talking about our lives. She was in a transition, having recently left her job of six years at a renewable energy company in Germany. She'd been biking around Central America from rural village to rural village as something of a vacation buffer (8). She was nearing the end of her trip and was about to dive into a job search back at home. The discussion was refreshingly honest for a conversation with someone new.

The next day, my friend and I were talking about it and we realized how real the conversation had become. He asked—how do you ask better questions? We began to analyze our conversation from the night before.

Here is what most people expect in a typical interaction:

1. Person A tells a story.
2. Person B listens while thinking about a story that proves to person A that he knows what he is talking about. He interjects and tells his story.
3. Person A does the same thing, listening in order to come up with another story of her own. The conversation stumbles forward.

Both parties are only partly listening and mostly occupied with telling stories that prove expertise, character, or knowledge.

What was different about our dinner conversation was that none of us felt the need to prove anything with our stories. The pressure to interject and to prove sits on a spectrum that we often rely on intuitively. On one side of the spectrum is proving and on the other side is sharing. Where we fall on this spectrum affects the quality of the questions we ask. We have become adept at knowing whether someone is proving or sharing.

Proving		Sharing
Speaking to build up your ego	vs.	Speaking for the benefit of those around you
Prioritizing the quantity of ideas	vs.	Prioritizing the quality and relevance of ideas
Speaking more than listening	vs.	Listening more than speaking
Showcasing what you know	vs.	Seeking to learn
Gaining confidence through others' affirmation	vs.	Gaining confidence from work done in private

The next time you're in a conversation, ask yourself if you're proving or sharing. Where do you fall on the spectrum between the two and what does this moment demand?

I came to understand this personally by doing the opposite. I was set to meet an academic at the forefront of research on black holes who was working on a project involving solar sails. I wanted to hold my own in the conversation. I wanted to show him what I knew.

I spent the week before reading, exploring the Internet, and researching articles about solar sail technology, and I even tried to get through *A Brief History of Time*. I got through two chapters and stopped, figuring I knew more than the average person. I wasn't planning on telling him that I had done any work whatsoever. With all my preparation, I went into the conversation wanting to show off my knowledge. I wanted him to turn to me and say, "You are really smart. Wow, you get it."

Instead of that reaction, I got something of the opposite. Within the first ten minutes I worked in all the stories I could that showcased everything I had learned and the opinions I had read. He barely acknowledged it. He just shrugged and continued telling me about where the technology was today and where the potential breakthroughs were. The whole conversation consisted of him telling me what *he* didn't know, and that there were only a handful of researchers around the world who were actually working on these problems right now.

I treat that conversation as a reminder and justification for always entering the world with an open mind, because the reality is that there's always more to know. It is what the Buddhists call "beginner's mind" and it is a bedrock of cultivating a lasting sense of curiosity that leads directly to unexpected opportunities, new knowledge, and even new jobs.

STUCK

MAKE YOUR OWN FINISH LINE

Nonlinear careers today often don't have finish line moments. We don't stay long enough with one company to get the golden watch, and the pace of change demands that as soon as one project is finished, another is there to take its place.

Finish lines are important. They help us mark and feel progress. They are the moment that we pause to consider the work we have done and celebrate with those who have helped us get there. In nonlinear careers, the need to create our own finish lines is even more acute. We are each running our own race, albeit with the help of others. The responsibility for marking the moments that matter falls on us.

Finish lines can be anything. I had a finish line bush in the Mission District in San Francisco. It was a simple jade plant that had just begun to show its red buds, and I only crossed it once. I woke up the morning after I arrived in town and had a call with some clients I had been working with for the last six months, helping to find a CEO for the company they were starting. They had finally signed the deal. They were clients I had taken on without knowing if I could do the job they'd asked me to do. It was a new industry, and the work demanded a lot of rigor and learning a new set of industry jargon. I was excited by it and had thrown myself fully into the task.

The moment I got off the call I felt a sense of relief and quiet accomplishment. The clients were already jumping forward into the next stream of work, the next person they needed me to hire, the onboarding, the next company, the next, the next . . .

I wanted to extend that feeling. I wanted to resist the "next thing." I had done something I'd had doubt about, that I didn't know how I was going to accomplish. I felt a sense of guilt for wanting recognition. I didn't want to ask for it—that defeated the whole purpose. Maybe they just didn't know how finish line worthy this moment was.

Still lost in thought, I put on my running gear and went for a four-mile run around the new neighborhood to get my bearings. As I ran, I thought about the last six months and all the work I had done, about the other areas in my life that had also changed over that time. This moment also included more personal milestones about letting go of relationships and finding a new rhythm. Even just being in San Francisco held special importance for me—I had booked the flight a day before to fly across the country to do work with a friend, and I was excited. I'd dreamed for years about one day being able to make a decision like that—to be able to fly at the last minute was a concept so alien from the way that I grew up, and being able to do it felt like a major accomplishment. I felt like I couldn't tell my friend. She might think I was overreacting and that it would be a little too much to celebrate something as small as the beginning of a new work relationship. What would she know about what it meant to me to fly across the country? It was another one of those small unspoken goals I had quietly held for years.

All of these feelings were running through my mind as I jogged around the streets of San Francisco. As I rounded the corner and closed in on the place I was staying, I saw the small jade bush. It was to be my finish line. I put all those feelings into it as I ran down the block. This was a moment to remember. I ran. I put my arms up as I passed the bush and I thought about the last six months and what I had finished and what it meant to be right here.

I could have waited for someone to recognize this moment—but the reality is that no one really knew the full scope of what this meant to me except myself.

I sat on the steps, tired from the run, and felt grateful. It was an important pause before the inevitable workload of the next steps of the job came in. I recognized and marked those six months of hard work that paid off with the clear finish line right behind me. As strange as it may sound, the finish line bush, the forty-five-minute run, and those few minutes on the stairs did just that. It was enough.

We need to create our own finish lines to help us mark when things go right. To free us from the expectation and waiting that we do for other people to tell us we are doing a good job or doing the right thing. These are personal moments that we can recognize. These moments will feed the momentum you need to get the next job.

THE EXERCISE

1. Choose a moment that is finish line worthy. Not all moments deserve a finish line. The more time and work that resulted in this moment, the better. Choose something you have already accomplished and give this act the weight it deserves.
2. Carve time away from your ordinary routine for your finish line moment. This will help your celebration stand out in your memory so you can reflect on the newness of your accomplishment.
3. Think about all the small moments that led up to this one large accomplishment. What exactly are you rewarding yourself for? What is it that you wish someone could recognize in you? What work have you done that is worth celebrating?
4. Mark the moment with something physical. Do you like to run, dance, or swim? What would a finish line dance look like? Maybe it is a combination of a powerful pose in a very special place. By marking the moment with action, not only will you know the joy of the finish line mentally, you will also experience it in your body.

5. Actually do it. Take the time, set it up, and follow through.
6. A way of extending the feeling of success is to take a picture of your finish line moment. Put the photo up in a place that you see regularly or share it with the most important people in your life. Whenever you look at the photo, even if it is just a bush on the side of the road, you will remember all the work you did and the feeling of accomplishment will come flooding back.

WHAT'S NEXT?

→ Learn about your center of gravity (27)
→ Make structural changes to your living space (50)
→ Decide how much you want to make and what is enough (212)
→ Schedule a vacation buffer (8)

SEND A "LOOKING FOR A JOB" E-MAIL TO FIVE CLOSE FRIENDS

You're crossing a threshold the moment you turn to a friend and vocalize that you have been unhappy at your work. You are ready for change. Feelings you may have been feeling for months are now out in the world—you have begun down a different path.

You have two choices in this moment. Either you settle into a rhythm of unhappiness at your job and continue complaining about it for the next five years, or you choose to do something, to take the first step.

When you choose to commit to changing, things shift slightly. There is a little more space between the everyday stress of the job and your identity. The office looks different, out of sync with the way you're feeling. Take some time to notice this feeling and make note of the differences. This feeling is a sign that you are on the right path.

This is the moment that you need to send a "looking for a job" e-mail, beginning with five friends that are closest to you. Sending this e-mail is a simple action that both solidifies the commitment you are making to yourself and begins the process of opening yourself up to possibilities that were impossible to imagine when the conversation was just in your head.

This is not the moment to send the e-mail to everyone you know—

just a few people is enough for now. The e-mail leaving your in-box is a commitment to starting a journey with emotional ups and downs. These feelings are manageable and they will actually guide you toward the exercises you need to do most.

Sending e-mails out to close friends can expand what you see as possible for yourself and will immediately widen your job prospects. Friends will refer you to friends looking for someone just like you. Before you send these, there are several important things to remember that will help ensure you get useful advice.

- **Ask the questions that you want the answers to.**

  People will give the advice that you ask for. If you begin by complaining, they will echo your energy and reconfirm your complaints, magnifying the negative. Make sure you have considered your sense of gravity (27) and its impact on how you're interpreting what friends tell you prior to accepting their opinion as fact.

  If there are specific questions that seem obvious but feel vulnerable, you don't need to ask for opinions on them just yet. Sit with them a little longer. It's okay to ask questions that you already believe you have an answer to as long as you are open to changing your opinion and gaining new insight. The questions you ask of friends are up to you. You don't need to invite everyone into your most private deliberations. Keep some on the periphery and let the select few into the most emotional things you are considering.

  Eventually, you should ask questions in person or on the phone. The e-mail is simply a stepping-stone to get to the real value—the conversation.

- **People will always tell you to do what they do.**

  The more passionate people are about their own work, the more tempting it can be to believe that the answer to your next step is doing what they do. Keeping this in mind, remain grounded and don't automatically assume they are right. This doesn't mean you shouldn't listen to them. Just know that most people tell you what has worked for them, and that won't necessarily also work for you.

Check in with yourself after your conversation and make note of the ways these friends live their life, and factor in the things that are specific to them, such as risk tolerance or life priorities.

- **Give yourself permission to ignore most of the advice.**

  You should listen and be open to learning from all advice, but this doesn't mean that you have to implement it, nor does it mean that you have to argue against it. You can listen and learn without doing either. You should take the mash-up approach to advice— compiling the pieces that seem relevant to you and reconstructing the individual pieces, stories, and ideas into something that matches the shape of your nonlinear career path.

- **Make sure to separate what you want from the path that you want to walk.**

  If you haven't already—read and decide on your own path (31). Once you understand your own path, it is easier to filter other people's advice. When you open yourself up to others, the advice they give you will be an unsorted mix of methods and experiences. Making sure you are clear on how those would fit for you will help you sort out what advice to pay attention to and what to graciously listen to and ignore.

These four points are constant reminders and practices to keep in mind as you begin to send out your e-mail to friends. Remember— adapt and adjust based on your own needs and relationships. You are the one who knows best the people you are sending this to. Often a quick text message to close friends can be easier than the more formal e-mail below.

THE EXERCISE

1. Choose five friends who are close to you and whom you respect professionally.
2. Send each friend an individualized e-mail requesting a meeting to talk about your career. Feel free to use this template:

> I am looking for my next gig at the intersection of *x, y,* and *z.* I haven't left yet, but I'm ready to wrap up my time at _____ company doing _____. Would love to chat with you and fill you in on what I'm thinking about and hear the latest from you.
>
> It would be great to catch up.
>
> —You

3. If you want to add more specific details, you can talk about the results of your career path, or try out one of your new ways of introducing yourself (126).
4. Here are a few great questions to get the conversation started when you are meeting with someone who knows you and your career trajectory well:
   a. From your perspective, what do you see me doing?
   b. How could my skills be put to use in the industry that you inhabit?
   c. I want to work at the intersection of *x, y,* and *z.* What opportunities come to mind that would be suited for me?
5. When you are meeting someone who doesn't know your career path well, consider the questions related to contacting someone you don't know (115) or interviewing someone (34).
6. After a few of these meetings, ask yourself, "What is the caliber of people I am being introduced to? What am I learning during each meeting? Am I doing most of the talking or am I mostly listening?"

Make any necessary changes to your questions and the people you e-mail next based on your feedback.

WHAT'S NEXT?

→ Help five people in your network (102)
→ Deal with jealousy (20)
→ Work on your ideal company list (119) and build out a company brief (78)

FIND A JUST-AHEAD MENTOR

WHO HASN'T DREAMED that some seasoned, generous, expert type would see something in you and give you that career-making job? You would have to do the work, but it would be clear, simple, and guaranteed to work. I am sure these moments exist (at least in movies), but you can't wait for them or manufacture the moment that leads to them. It would be akin to playing the lottery as a retirement plan.

An alternative does exist that is in your control, that is more common and in many ways more immediately helpful: find an individual five years ahead of you in his or her career and treat this person as a peer, but with the reverence of a mentor.

These just-ahead individuals are the ones who are close enough to the reality of your circumstances that they still directly engage with the opportunities that you need when you are on the hunt. They are closer to the ins and outs of the decisions you make—they are like peers or collaborators.

In 2016, I began a side project that had been a dream of mine since I was a child. I started a library. A local bookstore was closing down, and after a month of showing up every day choosing books, I made a deal with the owner and ended up with three thousand books stacked in boxes in my small one-bedroom apartment.

Three weeks later, the books were still there waiting and my brother came over and brought me back to reality. He noticed that my floor was sinking. There was a small crack between the window frame and the ceiling and the floor in my hundred-year-old building had shifted one inch below the baseboards.

I had to do something. I reached a point where something needed to change.

A few days later, I had a coffee with my friend Sabrina, who had reached out for job advice. We met at a coffee shop and inevitably, as almost anyone who met me last year could tell you, I started talking fairly quickly about the library, my month with the bookstore owner, and my sinking floor.

She interrupted me and said, "I have a library and no books." Sabrina ran the Made in NY Media Center by IFP, a twenty-thousand-square-foot incubator and coworking place. She and her team had built a small library and lounge in the back of their industrial space and had even built out the shelves, but they had run out of budget to buy books.

"Well, I have books and no library," I said.

It was a perfect match.

Two days later, a moving truck came to my apartment and picked up all the boxes and moved them into the space—it was the beginning of the shape of my library. I had envisioned a bright sunny space above the chaos of Chinatown with a big wooden table. It would be a place that people could visit and where I could write. But what I ended up with was this postindustrial, red-carpeted space with no natural light in Dumbo, Brooklyn. It was perfect.

I tentatively stepped into calling it a library. I came up with a whole list of reasons why it wasn't a real library. I didn't have enough books for it to be considered a real library. The space was donated and I wasn't paying for it. It wasn't real because the collection was built largely from one source. I even assumed that because my ideal vision included a space with natural light and the one I wound up with didn't, it wasn't worthy of the library title. I thought people wouldn't take it seriously. When people came to visit I was afraid they would think that I was just decorating my life with books, fetishizing a lifestyle that wasn't mine.

And then I met Andrew Beccone. He was a few years ahead of me in the library world. He is the founder of the Reanimation Library, currently housed in the Queens Museum. After a few people had told me about him, I decided to pay a visit. Andrew's library held some fifteen hundred to two thousand books in a back room of the museum. It was a windowless and plantless space with the books held along one wall in a blue metal shelving unit. Andrew was using the space for free. Despite all of this, I couldn't deny that this felt like the real thing—a real library.

All of my hesitations and insecurities vanished and I knew what I was doing was both real and valuable. Andrew's library had been treated seriously—he had done pop-ups at the Museum of Modern Art and had been invited around the world to discuss the library, all without any windows or plants in his space. How I saw Andrew in this moment was the same way someone would see me if I owned what I was doing—if I didn't pass it off as just collecting books. There was no difference between us other than time he had already put in, the work that I was excited to begin.

I had no more excuses. I named my library the Sorted Library. It was as real as the last couple of hours I had just spent in a back room at the Queens Museum. I couldn't even explain all this to my friend in the car on the way home. I felt blindsided by the experience. Things had changed so fast, and all I could think about was all of the work I was eager to do.

You don't need to know a mentor that well for it to be an important interaction. It doesn't need to be an equal relationship—sometimes the other person doesn't even need to know.

To help you find that just-ahead mentor right in front of you it can help to do the following exercise.

THE EXERCISE

1. Choose three people that you look up to for specific qualities. They can represent character traits or elements of the career that you want. Describe each of these characteristics in detail, adding or making up traits to fill in any gaps in your knowledge. Choose people based on your perceptions about what they represent.

2. Take all these details and pretend they are gathered in one person. What would this person's bio look like? Where would this person work? What would he or she be doing day-to-day? Ascribe percentage values to all the characteristics that this fictional mentor would have. Creating a fictional mentor helps you identify unexpected individuals who are just-ahead mentors.

3. Reflect on this fictional bio and make a list of all the places that this ideal person would be. If the fictional being you've created would be someone who is unapproachable, then ask yourself where this person would be at your age or stage. Where would this person be when he or she was just beginning? What roles would this person have? Where would he or she work? The closer the person you find is to your current reality, the better a just-ahead mentor this person will be.

WHAT'S NEXT?

→ Interview someone, seeking to understand the behind-the-scenes story of his or her career (34)
→ Consider the balance between physical and mental work that you have in your life (187)
→ Deal with feelings of jealousy (20)

RECORD YOURSELF IN A STRESSFUL SITUATION

Do you know that "in over your head" moment, when your heart starts to race, you begin to sweat, and your mouth dries up as you try to form words you only half believe? This exercise prepares you for that moment.

Two years ago, I was sitting beside someone I respected; I was perhaps overly attached to his opinion of me. I was overthinking everything, trying to ask insightful questions and demonstrate that I knew what I was talking about without coming off as arrogant. I wanted this person to work with me again, to turn to me and say, "Dev, we would love you to come and consult on other projects with us."

Unfortunately that didn't happen. Instead, I walked away from the conversation feeling like I had strung together sentences that barely made any sense. I would start a sentence only to discover what I was saying halfway through. It was unbearable. I had been in situations with this fellow before, when I'd reacted the same way, so this time before I walked into the meeting I set my phone to record and put it on the table during the whole ten-minute conversation.

I couldn't listen to it when I walked out of the room. I couldn't relive the experience. A month later, after finding the audio file on my computer, I decided I would include it in a whole batch that I was sending to a transcription service.

A week later, I read the transcript of that nerve-wracking conversation, expecting a sinking feeling. It didn't come. I read it all. It felt like an impartial conversation between Speaker One and Speaker Two that had nothing to do with me.

The sentences that I'd barely strung together made sense, and surprisingly what I realized was that the guy I was speaking with was hardly listening to me. I was so nervous the day of that conversation that I didn't notice he was trying to prove that he knew what he was talking about more than he was paying attention to anything I was saying.

I began editing that transcript on my computer, strengthening some of my arguments and even rewriting some of my answers. I spoke them aloud and repeated them until I could feel my voice in this new conversation.

This practice was transformative and sparked a simple habit that has become a source for constant learning. Recording yourself like this is the same practice that athletes, actors, speakers, and dancers do regularly. Even though we don't perform on stages or in stadiums in front of thousands, we owe it to ourselves to do the same thing.

THE EXERCISE

1. Choose a situation that makes you feel nervous, afraid, or concerned about how it will go.
2. Turn on your phone and record the conversation or interaction. You will be the only one who will be using it.
3. Don't listen to the recording. Hearing one's own voice in a stressful moment is unsettling.
4. Get the recording transcribed or pair up with a friend and transcribe each other's recordings for free.
5. Review and analyze. Rewrite sections you don't feel good about.

When did you act defensive, switch tones, or speak when you should have been listening? Read some of these parts out loud and pretend you are someone else. Cut out words that are unnecessary and look for patterns in the way you are speaking that make you feel good. Highlight those sections and look for places in the transcript where you could do more of this. Think about yourself as a professional athletic coach reviewing game-day footage, analyzing and tweaking the smallest moves. You can learn as much about the person you are dealing with as you can about how you react in different situations. Simply paying attention will transform how you come off in interviews or any situation where you need to be performing at your best.

WHAT'S NEXT?

→ Look for moments in the transcript that could teach you about mimicking a new way of being (43)
→ Spend some time describing your dream job and the path you want to take to get there (31)
→ Test a new type of decision-making process (205)

WIN OVER SOMEONE WHO CAST YOU ASIDE

As you meet more people, there will be some who will ignore you, who don't respond to your e-mails, or who seem disconnected or perpetually distracted. One of the reasons many of us don't push ourselves to reach out and talk to someone we don't know is because we're afraid this will happen. The lack of response can reconfirm our underlying belief that we aren't enough. It is also one of the reasons why we often feel stuck.

Don't rush to blame. Most people wish they could be more present, weren't so easily distracted, or had more time. But they haven't set up their life for this, and as a result they are unintentionally rude.

There is an antidote to this rudeness. This exercise reframes what you are doing so you stop thinking about each individual negative outcome and start thinking about it as a challenge: win over someone who has cast you aside.

Choose one person you feel it would be useful to talk to but who has been ignoring you. The goal is to use the following strategies to build trust, to stand out, and to get this person back on your side.

1. Remember an idea this person told you and demonstrate to him or her that you not only listened, but took action because of it. Once you follow through on that advice, send the person two e-mails.
2. In the first e-mail, make a small commitment, like visiting a place the person mentioned in your original conversation. In the second e-mail, write a thank-you note saying that you followed through on your commitment and wanted to give an update and get the person's advice on what you should do next.

These messages will be slightly different each time. The more attached you are to a person's response, the more you should rely on the exercise. Having a process enables you to get unstuck and stop thinking in circles. Most people never follow up when a message goes unanswered, so just by trying, you will set yourself apart in a meaningful way.

For individuals you are reaching out to for the first time, limit yourself to three tries. Make a commitment to let the person know the results of your action and then send one last e-mail three weeks later. If you get no response, then it's time to let it go and move down your job search spreadsheet (170).

This exercise gives you agency. It puts the power back in your hands. Following through on commitments also strengthens your own confidence and builds a sense of momentum that can break you out of a lull in your job search.

THE EXERCISE

1. Identify a person who has been ignoring your e-mails.
2. Send the person an e-mail where you make a commitment that is not dependent on the person's response, such as researching a topic that he or she mentioned to you or that you learned about as a result of his or her work. Repeat your primary request, such as setting a time for a meeting.

3. If you haven't heard from the person after two weeks, send a second, follow-up e-mail, letting the person know that you have followed through on your commitment and describing any outcome or insight you gained as a result. Thank him or her and repeat your primary request.
4. If you get no response, then it's time to let it go and move on to the next opportunity.

WHAT'S NEXT?

→ Add someone you've won over to your list of twenty people (99) and consider this person as a potential future boss (130)
→ Renegotiate five commitments that you have been putting off (59)
→ Situate yourself in a broader context, putting all of these e-mails in perspective (63)
→ If you are feeling hyperconfident, start work without telling the company (209)

SWITCH PLANS

PLANS CHANGE. Reality shifts. How do you know when it is worth reconsidering and going in a different direction? When do you accept the new reality and switch plans?

Charlene has a quiet sense of humility that was evident the moment I met her. She was finishing her executive master's program, had just finished a project consulting with Planned Parenthood, and was commuting from Singapore to New York each month for school while maintaining her life in Singapore and her job there as a vice president at an investment bank.

Charlene was raised in the small town of Monticello, New York, by two working-class parents who had immigrated from Colombia in the late 1960s. She grew up in a bustling Latino community that was centered on the resorts that would cater to people escaping the city.

She always had an inner calling to go abroad, but didn't know how to do it. At sixteen, she tried to convince her parents to let her study abroad, but it took two more years of convincing before they let her travel to Thailand as part of the American Field Service. Her experience away from home buoyed her into eventually attending an international relations program in Switzerland.

In Switzerland she diligently worked toward her goal of working in international relations. She learned a new language, took a job with the head of the program, and would wake at five a.m. to file papers at an investment firm to pay her bills along the way. After several years, in school, interning at the United Nations, and earning a master's in London, her dream opportunity emerged—going to do direct fieldwork in Afghanistan. It was the real work that she had always wanted. This felt like a once-in-a-lifetime opportunity and she had a couple of weeks to make the decision.

She began to phone mentors, talk with her family, and do her own research. As a week passed, the conversations all gave her the same message—don't take the contract. It didn't come with rest and relaxation breaks, which was a standard for work in war zones; there was no guarantee of it turning into a full-time job; and her mentor told her there would be a high chance that this particular contract would leave her disillusioned. She had to make a decision. Her family, who had been patient and trusting with her up to this point, didn't want her to go. On one hand was the opportunity and life she had been working for and on the other was an unknown future.

After a phone conversation with her sister, who tried to convince her to stay, the totality of evidence converged and convinced her to turn it down. She decided not to go. The reality had shifted.

It wasn't easy. It wasn't all of a sudden better. It took two years for her to reconcile her decision and find a new path; and yet ten years later she told me how turning down that opportunity had led her career in unexpected ways, through international institutions in Dubai, Oman, and finally New York. It was a career she wouldn't have given up for anything. These decisions are the hardest ones to make. When circumstances, life, and the reasons why you all of a sudden change, you have to put trust in yourself and walk away. You have to reground yourself in the work and adjust your expectations, making way for the next thing.

There is a tension between being headstrong and taking risks.

A few years earlier at a conference, I had witnessed a conversation about risk between a base jumper and an extreme athlete. The base jumper talked about how he didn't think about risk the same way that most of us do—it was all calculated. He had spent thousands of hours understanding and learning the physical limits of his body, his skills, and his equipment. He would combine this knowledge with the analysis his team would do on the physics, the weather, and the environment affecting any given jump. To him, risk meant certainty, knowing the exact margin that he had to work in. Risk was what enabled him to know that if one factor changed, it was a simple decision—don't move forward.

Moments like these become sources of deep confidence in ourselves. We will be confronted with these moments at times we least expect. Knowing that we can accept the change, draw on resiliency, make new plans, and remain focused is grounding.

THE EXERCISE

If you feel like you are coming up to one of these major life decisions and are feeling hesitant about the choices ahead, do the following steps to reground yourself and help you know when you are ready to switch plans.

1. Do some research on your options. What information can you gather to move from risk to certainty? Who can you talk to? What analysis can you do or have others do that will provide you with more data?

2. List all of the contributing factors at play when you make a decision. This could include your mental state, your family's opinions, the political situation, or the advice of someone you care about. What can you do to identify other factors that might affect your decision? Is there other research you can do? Are there other people you can ask for objective opinions?

3. Write down all of these contributing factors on a scorecard. Tally

your scorecard, rating each factor on your list on a scale of one to five: one being unfavorable and five being highly favorable.

4. Between the time you make your initial decision to right before you say yes or no, review your scorecard and take note of any factors that have changed. If these changes show you that this decision is now beyond your own personal margin of safety, walk away and switch plans.

WHAT'S NEXT?

→ Sit quietly in a room for forty-five minutes (54)
→ Revisit your runway and financials, making adjustments for this new plan (12)
→ Go on a solo trip (40) or if necessary schedule a vacation buffer (12)
→ Rethink your daily routine (57)

FIELD NOTE: LIVING WITH LESS

SOMETIMES IT TAKES LONGER than expected to get a job. In these cases, you may need to extend how long you can keep your momentum going and find ways to prolong your bank balance. Living with less is the best way to do that quickly. The practice of living with less, even when it may not be a necessity, can make you at ease in many areas of your life. There is a joy and a sense of fulfillment that stems from applying the Buddhist economics framework that we are going to learn here.

My friend Patricia was leaving town to travel for four months, and in the frenetic rush of getting ready and preparing her place for Airbnb guests, she moved the majority of her clothes and stuff into a storage locker and decided to pack only what she could fit in a carry-on. Four months went by, which she spent traveling to Italy, South Africa, Greece, and Hungary, and when she returned home, she unpacked her bag and picked up where she left off. A week went by before she realized what had changed.

She had fallen back into a home routine and didn't miss any of her things she had left in storage. She had experienced living with less as a result of her travels and the effects rippled through her life. She began to save more money, spend less time shopping on weekends, and was more mindful of all the ways that she was using resources beyond money, including her time.

Buddhist economics is founded on the question "What is the least amount of resources, work, and toil needed to achieve your given intention?" The question doesn't prescribe judgment or say that you should stop going out to nice restaurants or forgo spending for a whole month. It just asks you to question first.

For example, lunch. If you are trying to take a potential employer to lunch to impress him or her, then the least amount of resources, work, and toil may mean going for a lunch at an expensive restaurant. It is the easiest way to achieve your given intention. If, on the other hand, you're at home working diligently on a project and you want to remain focused, the easiest way to achieve your given intention may mean that you make a simple salad or reheat leftovers from the night before. The appropriate action for the right intention.

Jake had a job that—at least on paper—seemed like his dream position. He worked as an art director at an ad agency that worked on social-mission-driven campaigns. But even though the job looked perfect, he still wasn't happy—the job didn't satisfy his desire to work and build with a community of creative people like him.

He left the job and committed himself to trying something different. He doubled down on a project he had started called You're Better than Brunch, began freelancing with groups he cared about, held a gallery show with his artwork, and lived life as an artist. He also checked off some big life milestones, including marriage and honeymoon. After almost a year of this lifestyle, he realized he had to make a change financially—he was gaining momentum, but he was overspending. He was ready for a rhythm change (57). He wanted a job.

He decided to try an experiment. For the month of November, he wouldn't spend money on anything apart from groceries and a few subscriptions like Netflix. A few months earlier, he had done a no-sugar month, so he applied the same logic and game structure to this challenge: no-spend November.

The first two weeks were hard. He was turning down invitations to things he would have readily gone to and paid money for, like nights out and events, and then he started reframing and being more proactive. He invited couples over to his house for dinner—they would cook together and spend hours talking. The conversations were more intimate in a home setting—friends understood and began inviting themselves over. He had found a simple way to create a space for real, meaningful conversation.

As the month closed, he and his wife went out for dinner at their favorite spot to celebrate. They had each spent less than $100 the whole month. They went back to spending money, but things had shifted and they asked themselves a different set of questions before blindly saying yes to going out. They asked themselves what they wanted—if they wanted that intimate evening in with another couple or a night out. It was a new type of decision that they hadn't considered before. This new perspective gave them a sense of resilience. They now knew that if they were making a transition, they could last much longer than they previously had expected.

Buddhist economics works on small and big decisions alike. You have the opportunity to practice these decisions daily. Every decision, from what to eat to what you should do next, can be an opportunity to practice the two-part question: What is my intention? And what is the least amount of work, resources, and toil I could use to achieve it?

APPLYING FOR JOBS

GO TO A JOB BOARD
AND THEN LEAVE

JOB BOARDS SHOULD BE a last resort when looking for a job. Although this seems counterintuitive, only 3 percent of all jobs are found by applying through a job board, so you may as well invest your time doing something else. The biggest unforeseen cost to beginning the lengthy process of applying on job boards is the emotional dive you take when you send applications out into the unknown only to hear nothing in response.

No matter how qualified you are, the lack of a response can make you question your skills and feel like the work you have put in up to this point has not been worth it. This is not true. You are already in the middle of your nonlinear career path (3), and the work does count. Blame it on the job board.

As a recruiter, I can tell you that about 70 percent of the jobs that I hire for change the job description during the hiring process—companies often learn what they need through talking with prospective employees. This is just one reason why you may not hear back. It often has nothing to do with your application or your skill set, and yet it's hard to avoid internalizing the lack of response when applying online as being directly about you. As a candidate you don't know if they are actively hiring or if they're posting a job even though they're likely to hire internally. You don't know the team, the place, or the shifting nature of the job description.

The other tendency you have to combat when applying on job boards is mission creep. As you click through job after job, they start to blend together and before you know it, you're applying for jobs that you're only marginally interested in. You get caught up in the act of winning or getting an interview instead of making active choices about what you want your next job to be. Imagine picking your career based on the same algorithm that picks the next YouTube video that you watch. You are better than that. You have agency.

Use this sense of agency. Jobs come from meeting with people (112), learning new things (82), and being engaged and in pursuit of ideas that excite you (75). They come from being out there in the real world "doing." Pick at random from any of the activities in this book—it will be a better use of your time.

Job boards do have their uses. They can be used to find a job title (176), as a source of ideas when you are writing your own job description (200), or even as a method of discovering companies you didn't know about (78). If you do come across a job that you are actually interested in, find your future boss (130) and send an e-mail to the company you want to work for (184) before you apply blindly online.

THE EXERCISE

1. Visit a job board.
2. Leave immediately.
3. Open this book at random and do that activity instead.
4. Send this chapter to a friend who is spending too much time on job boards.

WHAT'S NEXT?

→ Cultivate your sense of curiosity and learn to ask better questions (133)

→ Rethink your daily routine (57)

→ Map your career path and study your moments of transition (3)

ORGANIZE YOUR JOB SEARCH IN A SPREADSHEET

WHETHER SOMEONE RESPONDS TO YOU or not is out of your control. What you do control is how many companies you reach out to and what you ask. Paying attention to the wrong information can cause you to lose the momentum you may already have. Creating a job search spreadsheet is a structured way to ensure you stay focused on what matters.

The spreadsheet will remind you of what is in your control, and it will give you a nonemotional perspective on your progress. Managing your emotional state during a job search regardless of whether or not you currently have a job can be the difference between getting a new job in three weeks or in six months.

Begin by including every potential opportunity as a distinct line on a spreadsheet. This could be a person you met (126), a company you identified (119), or an opportunity that you found via searching in an unfamiliar place (90). In addition to recording the opportunity, you should assign each one a status, such as:

1. Setting intention
2. Reaching out
3. Initial meeting

4. Follow-up
5. Proposal/job application

Other columns that you may want to include could be who introduced you, next steps, or a priority column. Make the spreadsheet use-
able but not onerous. Your spreadsheet will start to take the shape of a
typical sales funnel, a pyramid with a wide base of cold opportunities
and a winnowing peak of a few that are in the proposal/job application
stage. This shape will help you understand that it is normal to have
twenty initial conversations and one potential interview. It is important
to remember that not all conversations need to have a tangible result to
be of value—some may start off as exploratory and turn into an opportunity later, or some may simply remain informative.

The goal of each interaction is to move the status forward one step
from reaching out to initial meeting, from initial meeting to follow-up.
As you begin to meet individuals, you may find you want to include
other stages, such as research or second meeting, that are related to your
particular industry.

The benefit of visualizing your progress in a funnel is that it prevents
you from expecting every conversation to turn into a job opportunity.

Focusing on your job search spreadsheet also stops you from pushing
too hard on any one opportunity at the wrong time. It is a visual reminder that when one opportunity is out of your control you have
other people or companies to focus on.

Thinking about your opportunities in such a strictly businesslike
fashion can feel cold and foreign. People become numbers moving
through a spreadsheet. But like much of the advice in the book, it's the
way that you approach this work that makes the difference. The struc-
tures are simply the form—it's up to you to fill them with the right
feeling. You need to ensure your conversations are grounded and your
interactions are not merely transactional but filled with respect and hu-
manity. The spreadsheet and form will only help you feel more emotionally in control as you enter the unknown.

THE EXERCISE

1. Create a job search spreadsheet and list all of your current or prospective opportunities.
2. Your goal for each meeting is to move the person one stage forward in the funnel. Personalize the spreadsheet for your own needs. Add stages for the job application process and spend time setting expectations for each stage.
3. After each meeting, record notes from the meeting and reflect on what you can do next in order to move the relationship forward.

A word of caution: This particular way of structuring your time shouldn't be applied early in the transition process. This is a later-stage activity. It is for when you have already done the work of understanding what you want to learn next and what path you want to walk. You need to know the questions that you want to pursue and you need to have made the shift from the in-between state to one of decisive action before this exercise can be useful for you.

WHAT'S NEXT?

→ If you are feeling financial pressure, consider freelancing or getting a side hustle (180)
→ Work on the story of yourself you are going to tell at interviews (191)
→ Renegotiate any commitments you have made throughout the job search process that you haven't followed through on (59)

TALK TO A RECRUITER

WHEN YOU ARE FIRST APPROACHED by a recruiter it can seem flattering, but more commonly it's an annoyance. Recruiters usually work with people seven or more years into their career, so if you have less experience than that you may want to skip this chapter; don't worry, you aren't missing much.

The annoying part is that the offers most people receive are disconnected from the reality of what they are looking for. The average recruiter doesn't understand nonlinear careers. Recruiters specialize in helping you get to the next logical step on a linear path. They aren't going to help you understand your future self (17) or help you reframe your story (191). At the end of the day, their bills are being paid by someone else. Remember, this is your journey, and you have everything you need to take control of your search yourself without relying on the arbitrary opinions of recruiters.

Another cause of discomfort in the interaction is the fact that there are so many unknowns on the other side of a LinkedIn message. It can feel like a first date but without the algorithms that dating companies have spent millions of dollars perfecting (and which still often lead to bad first dates).

When it comes to recruiters, you have to remember that you have the power. To take the first date analogy one step further, you have the ability to choose the meeting place you feel most comfortable in, you get to ask the first question, and you decide when to leave. You have the power.

If you do end up on the phone with a recruiter, try to understand the recruiter's relationship to the client and spend time getting him or her to explain the position the company is trying to fill. Seeking out this information will demonstrate that you value yourself and that you have healthy skepticism, which will signal to the recruiter that he or she needs to prove to you why you should be interested in this job.

As a recruiter myself, it is very rare that anyone puts me on the spot with questions as in-depth as the ones below. Ninety percent of candidates treat the initial conversation like an interview they didn't ask to do for a job they don't understand—which, in fairness, is what it typically is. Turning the conversation around and asking the recruiter questions will enable you to get a full understanding of the position on offer and give you the power to choose if it is a job opportunity that you would consider next.

THE EXERCISE

1. First, figure out the recruiter's relationship to the employer. The answers to the questions below will give you a good sense of how good this recruitment firm is, its relationship to the employer, and if it is a rigorous or more junior company that sends people indiscriminately forward. "Contingency" means that the recruiters only get paid if you are hired. "Retained" means they get paid regardless. There are pros and cons to both, but typically retained search firms are higher end.

   Ask your recruiter the following questions:

   Before you tell me the details about the job, would you mind telling me a bit about your relationship with the employer?

Is your firm on a retained search? Or is this search contingency based?

Have you hired anyone for this client before? For what roles?

What does the presentation of candidates to your client typically look like? What info do you include?

2. Then you can get into the particulars of the position. Here are a few further questions to ask that play off of the unique position a recruiter has in the hiring process.

How does what this client is asking for differ from what you think the company needs for this role?

What kinds of places has this client hired from before?

Have you presented the client with a short list of candidates yet? If so, how did that go and what did you learn about what the client wants?

What type of person do you think would be a good culture fit with the company, and what gives you the sense that I'd fit in?

And if you are feeling like you need a little ego boost:

Why is this company interested in my profile?

WHAT'S NEXT?

→ Update your LinkedIn profile as your future self (17)
→ Do some personal work and discover your personal gravity (27)
→ Create a company brief on the company that the recruiter was pitching you on (78)

FIND A JOB TITLE

FINDING A JOB TITLE and job description that resonate with you can help you clarify what you do and what you don't do. What tasks and skills fall in your domain and which help ground your dream job in reality. Job boards should be avoided when applying for jobs. They typically only work for linear careers that follow a defined path (167). However, they are a good place to do some general research.

We live in an era when tech companies and start-ups feature more and more made-up job titles that seem like magical mash-up jobs perfect for the nonlinear careerist. They elicit job envy and seem like a perfect fit made specifically for you. But if you dig a little deeper, what you will realize is that they are often very similar to jobs that have always existed, albeit selling a new type of product.

Miriam began her career as a diplomat for the Canadian government, working with Foreign Affairs Canada to help the department launch entrepreneurship accelerator programs out of the embassy in New York. After ten years, she decided she was tired of the administration at the time, the bureaucracy, and the pace of change in government, and she decided to take a sabbatical and start her own business teaching meditation. She transitioned to doing the work she had wanted to do, but after two years of the hustle, she was considering the stability of a job with a regular paycheck once again.

I asked her what job title she wanted. She said chief mindfulness officer. She had heard that these positions exist, and on the surface it seemed like she was perfectly qualified. We delved into it further by beginning to ask: Where did this job exist specifically?

She had spent a few years by this point in the mindfulness space attending conferences, and if there was anyone talking about mindfulness careers, she would have known about it. She could name only a small handful of companies that offered them, including Aetna, Google, and several small meditation studios. We dove into the specifics and what the responsibilities were for these jobs.

In some cases, the chief mindfulness officer was an updated version of a more traditional "people and culture" role. Team retreats, internal culture programming, talent onboarding, and the more traditional functions were being folded under this new title as a way to make a broader statement about company values. In other cases, the chief mindfulness officer was actually responsible for a specific profit center of the business—figuring out how to export the company's training for a fee to other corporations. In the case of the health insurance provider, the chief mindfulness officer would play a role on the preventative health team to reduce an individual's insurance needs.

When we talked about whether those tasks were actually what Miriam was interested in, the conversation was less enthusiastic. I tell this story not to discourage you or say it is impossible, nor to suggest that it's worthy to aim at having a job with an unorthodox job title, but rather to clarify what it means to get these jobs.

These jobs are undeniably out there and may even be on the rise, *but* considering that there are only a handful of examples, actually getting these jobs involves a rhythm similar to the entrepreneurial energy of a freelancer pitching to big corporations for consulting gigs. It involves meeting the right CEO, long lead times, pitching small engagements, understanding the company's needs, and then working with the employer to both name and create your own role—chief mindfulness officer. This is decidedly not the rhythm that Miriam and I talked about when we initially sat down. She wanted a job that was the opposite—something steady, meaningful, and more secure.

When you come across a job title that seems too good to be true, treat it as a jumping-off point or a new line of inquiry. Before you realign your career aspirations, ask the following questions:

- Do multiple people at multiple companies have this job title? Is it a title that is directly under the CEO or would it need CEO buy-in?
- What do they actually do? What are their responsibilities?
- What are the skills that one needs to develop to get there?
- How have the people in these positions gotten their jobs? Is there a common path they took, and how much of it has to do with relationships and being at the right place at the right time?

Finding a job title that is common on job boards can help you narrow down and understand more clearly what you want. Don't worry about the companies attached to these listings—for this exercise focus only on the title itself, the description, and the skills needed to thrive in it.

THE EXERCISE

1. Make a list of job titles. Search a job board and write down ten job titles that interest you.
2. Do your research to determine the reality of the work behind the job titles you have chosen. This could be done via interviewing people (115) or by working on a company brief (78). Continue this exercise using only the titles of the jobs that continue to resonate with you after you have done your research.
3. Even the job titles that may seem misleading often suggest ideas for skills that you can add to your to-learn list (72) or that can inform how you describe your mission fit (194). Update your to-learn list and add any interesting companies you come across to your job

search spreadsheet (170). For the job titles that you are interested in, make an inventory of the required, preferred, or desired skills listed in the job description. Cross-reference this list with your list of skills (69).

WHAT'S NEXT?

→ Find a future boss who has your ideal job title (130)
→ Learn something outside of school (82)
→ Map a network around someone who has a job title you want (105)

GET A SIDE HUSTLE

SOMETIMES YOU JUST NEED to make some money and give yourself more time to figure out what to do next, to learn a new skill (72), or to do the other work necessary to switch careers (158). Side hustles used to be synonymous with restaurant work, but today a new alternative has arrived. The sharing economy has emerged over the last five years to provide a new option for those looking for flexible employment that they can turn off or on based on their own needs.

Ride-sharing companies are the most common option, but there are also a host of other alternatives that continually come up. From renting out your place through a site like Airbnb when you are on a research trip (75) to doing manual labor or task organizing with a company like TaskRabbit, the sharing economy provides a chance for you to monetize a skill or simply trade your time for some dollars.

It is important to realize that there is a great deal of work involved in a side hustle, and there is no free money. In order to make enough money to sustain yourself, you have to have the drive and discipline to treat it as a job. Expenses and taxes are often left up to you as a contractor, and the incentive to work is solely based on your desire to put the time in.

This is not an easy job, but it is an accessible one. When taking on a side hustle, it is important to remember that you aren't stepping off your path—this is a part of it. I interviewed one woman who had been working in purchasing for more than nine years. She had taken the past eight months off to travel and recalibrate, since she wanted to change industries and the trajectory of her career. When I met her, her savings were running low and she was actively engaged in the job hunt. After changing a few things to live with less (162), she decided to pick up a few hours a day of driving to give herself just enough to pay the bills without side-tracking her search for a longer-term commitment to a more lucrative contract in her old industry. The side hustle kept her focused on the goal of transitioning into a new industry while helping her pay the bills.

It was a similar story for Emily, albeit at a different stage in her career. Emily was a recent graduate and had entertained a few job offers, but none of them felt right. She was wary of taking one of these first offers out of college in case it ended up defining her career before she had put the time into deciding what she wanted. She had been working at a local bar, but after a full shift she would get home exhausted at two or three in the morning. It left her no time to reflect and do the work to figure out what she really wanted to do. Emily knew driving wasn't a long-term career path for her, so the decision to begin was easy—it was a side hustle, a commitment that wouldn't alter the trajectory she would eventually choose to take. Taking a job in the sharing economy was the perfect placeholder that gave her enough time and mental space to figure out the next step.

THE EXERCISE

1. Review how long your money will last (12) in order to determine if a sharing economy side hustle will extend your runway.
2. Decide how many hours you want to commit to this side hustle. What time of day do you want to be working? How do you want to feel after your workday? Consider all these factors before deciding on your side hustle to help determine the best fit for you.

3. Investigate and weigh the pros and cons of all the sharing economy companies that you are most interested in. Look up "sharing economy companies" online to get the latest list of companies that fall under this umbrella term.

4. Weigh the pay-to-time ratio. The sharing economy space is littered with small companies actively trying to grow, many of which are fledgling and may not have significant uptake in your market. Stick with the larger ones that have a well-developed marketplace.

5. Start work and get paid. The cost of trialing a service is low. Try a few and measure them against the list of criteria that you settled on in step two. Make your decision, start working, and get paid.

CLARIFY EVERYDAY PURPOSE

When you take on a side hustle, there will be moments when you will question whether you are on the right path. The day-to-day isn't always fun. One way to deal with this is by re-grounding yourself in your everyday purpose, the tactical reason why you are doing the work you are doing.

When Julian was fourteen years old, his hockey coach in Toronto would give the team pep talks in the locker room before the game—"If you boys want to be more effective on the ice you have to constantly be asking yourself, 'What am I doing right now?' Are you waiting for the puck to come to you? Are you setting up a play?" There is always an answer, and you always have the opportunity to alter your course. What are you doing right now?

This question stuck with Julian, not only on the ice but in other aspects of his life as well. In his midthirties a few years after moving to a new city, Julian was feeling frustrated waiting on contracts he wasn't excited about to come through. One day he was standing in line at a federal building, waiting to register his family for subsidized health insurance, and he looked at his wife, scanned the room a couple of times, and the question came into his head—"What am I doing right now?"

He stepped out of the line and went home. He sat down with his wife and they confronted the reality of their finances and how their life had turned out since the move. Things weren't working as they'd expected, and ultimately they ended up moving back to Toronto.

Whenever you feel stressed or uncertain, ask yourself, "What am I doing right now?" It can be the reminder you need either to stay focused in pursuit of the longer-term goal or to reevaluate, as Julian did. The question will give you the confidence and perseverance to know what to do next. Write the question down somewhere visible, to remind yourself to pause and reflect throughout the day.

WHAT'S NEXT?

→ Apply Buddhist economics to your life and learn to live with less (162)
→ Take this side hustle as an opportunity to mimic a new way of being (43)
→ If you find yourself bored and questioning what you are doing, find interest in the details (94)

SEND THIS E-MAIL TO THE COMPANY YOU WANT TO WORK FOR

THIS E-MAIL IS A MAGIC BULLET. It follows a very specific format and will get you a meeting that will lead to your new job. The catch is, you need to actually have done the work to support the claims you make in this e-mail for it to succeed, and that takes a lot of effort.

If you skipped the rest of the book and came directly here, reading this chapter will give you a sense of why the work in the earlier sections of the book is so necessary. In order to write this e-mail from a place of authenticity you need to have considered your purpose (25), defined what you want to learn next (72), identified what skills you have to offer (69), and explored the different ways you can actually take action on a company's mission (194).

Consider this as a road map. If you do the work necessary to write this e-mail you *will* get a meeting and a job.

Companies get hundreds of resumes full of real skills but no mission; they also get job applicants bursting with a personal mission who have no skills. This e-mail works because it proves that you have both. Here are the four paragraphs necessary for this e-mail to work:

1. **Prove three ways that you have a real skill.**

   Companies need people with real skills. Choose a skill that you
   know the company needs, based on all the research you have done
   in your company brief (78). Companies need people with skills that
   are directly applicable to the real jobs they need done, like account-
   ing, project management, and design. Soft skills like leadership and
   willingness to learn don't count.

   If you don't immediately know how to prove that you have the
   skills they need, try the following exercises: make a list of your
   skills (69), make a list of what you want to learn (72), and take a
   course outside of school (82).

2. **Prove three ways that you are mission-aligned.**

   You must prove that you are committed to the mission of the company with tangible examples. Whether it's through the extensive
   interviews you have done with leaders in the field (115), sharing the
   results of a line of inquiry (90), or the volunteer experience that you
   did five years ago, show what you have done. You need to prove
   that you are mission-aligned, and that means much more than a
   one-liner at the top of a resume template.

3. **Say that you were going to do it yourself, but you can create a
   deeper impact by working with their company.**

   Tell them that you have been thinking, researching, and beginning
   to work in this field and then you found their company. Tell them
   that you realized their company is doing the same work or research
   that you had begun to do by yourself and how much more you
   could do if you worked together with them.

4. **Request an opportunity to talk.**

   Finally, in the last paragraph, ask for the opportunity to talk, get
   advice, and learn about how you can work together. Close the
   e-mail with a simple request. Always approach this request as though
   you are already doing this work. In the meeting itself, all you need

to do is iterate the ways that you have mission alignment and employable skills, and tell them that you want to find a role within their company where you can put all of this into action to bring the company value. It is rare that someone has put in the effort to make the claims you're making in this e-mail. You'll stand out from the crowd, and you're guaranteed to get a meeting.

Disclaimer: This e-mail takes a tremendous amount of work to ensure that it is authentic and effective. You have to commit to building and strengthening real skills and to becoming mission-aligned so that it's impossible to fake. If you are short on either mission or skills, employers will be able to tell and the e-mail won't work.

There is a pathway to get a job with the company that you want to work for, and this e-mail is one of the final steps. This is just a template, so treat it as a roughly hewn guide. Each e-mail you write should be unique and reflect the specific mission and purpose of the company. There are thousands of stories any one of us can tell of our experiences. If you need help putting the pieces of yours together in the right way for a particular situation, revisit the exercise on preparing your interview story (191). The employer won't do the work to understand your story, but you can, and the employer will not only notice but hire you because of it.

WHAT'S NEXT?

→ Take an action that demonstrates how mission-aligned you are (194)
→ Try out a new decision-making process so that you will be ready to choose the job you take next (205)
→ Keep your job search spreadsheet updated with all of the companies you are reaching out to (170)

FIELD NOTE: BALANCING PHYSICAL AND MENTAL WORK

To be in balance does not mean to be equal—a diet that consists of half fruit and half dessert is not a balanced diet. The balance of physical and mental work in anyone's life is personal yet important to understand as you navigate a job search and consider your next career. Neither is better than the other—they feed different parts of you.

I spent two weeks in a workshop at Arcosanti, an experimental urban laboratory two hours from Phoenix. The time was divided up into a mix of physical labor and lectures. During the morning I was given the task of mixing concrete—moving silt and sand from one location to another, and then loading a bucket of gravel, water, two buckets of sand, more water, and two more buckets of gravel into the mixer and adjusting until the concrete had the right slump.

I used to complain about doing this type of work whenever I went home to visit my parents. At home my mother would inevitably ask me to move compost around the yard in buckets and wheelbarrows, and I would respond with my standard litany of excuses. I remember thinking, as I pushed a wheelbarrow across the grounds at the workshop, that this time I had officially forfeited any excuse to avoid that work, since I'd flown across the country and paid a workshop fee to do the very thing I would try to get out of doing at home. And yet now I wanted to do the work. The work that I was doing was not a chore—I fell into a rhythm that felt natural. The routine enabled me to actually accomplish something with the others, while the lectures provided a reprieve when I was tired and eager to sit and listen. It was the right balance for me, for that moment in time.

Physical work helps us connect with our bodies. It is not solely the domain of hard labor—it also includes work like making the patterns for clothes, working on the details of an oil painting, or building furniture. These are all tasks with a strong connection between your work, your time, and what you produce. There is a focus that comes from the flow of physical work, the busyness, and the presence of mind you have to maintain when you are moving heavy boxes or navigating the bustle of a restaurant as a server. Time can move differently.

The goal is not to romanticize the realities of physical labor. It's hard. It is all-consuming, and it is often underpaid. But it's important to recognize that this work has a role in our lives. The routine of physical work can settle us. It is also something that can sustain us when we want to dedicate the remainder of our time to mental work.

Mental work provides a different type of engagement. Solving challenging problems, working out logical arguments, or navigating multiple competing interests can take all our focus and leave us just as tired but in need of a different type of rest.

Paying attention to the balance you have in your life can be instructive and point you toward opportunities that you would have otherwise overlooked. Moving between physical and mental work or seeking a job that is counter to how you currently spend your days can enable you to do more of what you love. One type of work can help you recharge from the other.

The balance you find for yourself will continue to shift throughout the duration of your life. Pay attention and recognize it; track these shifts and notice the patterns because they may point you toward what you should do next.

INTERVIEWING

PREPARE YOUR INTERVIEW STORY

PEOPLE GET HIRED when the story of their life connects with other people's and matches the skills of the job they are looking for. We bond by finding common ground and building from a shared place of understanding. It is the same way that we make friends and find partners—common ground can bring relief, connect us, and be personally rewarding. Sometimes this commonality can be the mission of the company or our skills, and other times it can be race, class, and privilege markers.

Although we don't have control over the stories society tells about us, we do have control over how we tell our own stories regardless of these types of markers. Our stories are not fixed—there are many ways to tell the same story while remaining grounded in truth. This is an exercise about retelling and reshaping your story by creating a portfolio or a simplified resume. It is an important skill that will help you do really well in an interview.

It is easy to have the expectation that interviewers should be able to understand your story as long as you share it all. The reality is that people won't be paying close attention, and it is not up to them to understand. It's up to you to explain. It's better that way, no matter how complicated or nuanced your story is or how far the interviewer's reality may be from yours. You have the control.

In order to start understanding how to retell your story, it can be helpful to think about the experiences and jobs you have had as a collection of Lego bricks, each with its own specific shape and color. The short internship may be a single green brick, and that four-year degree may look like three or four yellow bricks stacked up on each other.

Even small moments of learning, turning points, or any experience you deem worthy gets a shape and color. These shapes and colors make up your portfolio—who you are. Building out this portfolio could be an endless exercise, so begin by making a list of experiences that correspond to core values or skills that you hold close.

Each time we tell stories of our lives, we draw from our portfolio of Lego bricks, making various configurations of who we are. We often tell the same story with the same shape out of habit and familiarity.

In order to build trust and find common ground, you need to add in one extra step before you share your own story—uncovering the story shape of the person interviewing you.

Listen for this person's particular configuration of Lego bricks. In order to do this, you need to ask secondary questions, listen for similarities, and follow tangential paths—where the interviewer grew up, why he or she started doing this work, what he or she is reading—tangents that may lead you to uncover a story that resembles one of your own. This can also be done during the research phase prior to the interview. By bringing important moments in that person's life to the surface, you will reveal what makes the interviewer who he or she is and how his or her values were formed.

Once you understand the interviewer's story, it's up to you to look at your portfolio on the spot and tell a story of yourself that most closely matches theirs—one that contains similar shapes or similar colors. This often comes from omission, not addition.

Being able to do this on the spot in an interview takes some practice. Begin by limiting yourself to three different versions of your own personal story. For me, these would be Dev the recruiter, Dev the nonprofit executive director, and Dev the book lover. Three different stories that highlight different aspects of my personality and experience.

It will feel awkward initially to tell a different story of yourself. We are used to telling the same one over and over, so any aberration can feel foreign. As you get more skilled at reshaping your story on the spot, you realize that you can make subtle adjustments, substituting one story for another, all helping you to connect and meet people where they are at.

THE EXERCISE

1. Make a list of ten "Lego brick" experiences that you would include in your portfolio. Consider your nonlinear career map and try to include experiences that aren't currently in your story.
2. Write a short statement about each story so you are familiar with the purpose of each story and why you tell it.
3. Create three different combinations of your Lego bricks, constructing three different stories about yourself.
4. Find a friend to practice with and ask questions to uncover his or her story. Adapt and tell your story in a way that matches some of the color and shape of the story your friend told you.
5. Apply this method of telling your story to your resume and adapt and simplify your resume so you can use it for numerous different opportunities.

WHAT'S NEXT?

→ Go back and revisit how you described your dream job and compare it to your interview story (31)
→ Do your research on the company you are going to interview with by creating a company brief (78)
→ Think more creatively about your personal story and write fiction about yourself (37)
→ Update your LinkedIn profile as your future self (17)

PROVE YOU ARE
MISSION-ALIGNED

THIS IS ESPECIALLY IMPORTANT for individuals who are changing industries or making the move toward a company that does good in the world. Being mission-aligned means more than just wanting to do good—it's about understanding the nuances of the purpose of the company and demonstrating this understanding through action.

Mission fit is often confused with culture fit. Culture fit, although important, can sometimes be a proxy used for race or class divides. It can mean hiring people "like me" and actually function as an unspoken barrier. Being mission-aligned will actually help you hedge against this bias if you don't look or talk like the group you want to work with. It can buttress you against the fact that people hire people who are like themselves. Mission alignment that is developed with sincerity and integrity cuts through those often unsaid barriers to getting hired at a company you want to work for.

In order to get mission alignment, you don't need to have been working in an industry for years, nor do you need to have had a moment of self-revelation that led you to this one company. What you need is to demonstrate that when you say, "I believe in this company and want a job that aligns with my mission," it is true and authentic. It needs to be grounded in real action.

Even a small amount of work put into gaining a mission fit, spoken about honestly, will be clear when you begin talking to employers. It's easier than you imagine, but not as quick as just making it up. Companies will rarely call you out on the small white lie "I believe in your mission," so you could get away with it. But people know. When you have done the real work that demonstrates you are connected to the mission, you act differently, use different anecdotes, and deliver that single line with a different sense of confidence. It just takes a little more work and a deeper commitment to authenticity.

This type of authenticity will resonate more than overstated claims. It is also just a better way to be—it takes less mental work to reconcile who we are with who we say we are. This is why some of the actions in this chapter are small and simple—reading a book, attending a talk. These small actions will bring you small moments of insight that will give confidence and an authentic voice to your claim—I believe in your mission, I have been doing my work, and I want to work with you (184).

THE EXERCISE

There are endless ways to find mission fit. Here are several you can try:

1. Listen to a talk or read a book by a leader in the field.
2. Make a list of questions the industry needs to answer and attempt to answer them.
3. Go on a research trip (75).
4. Talk to people at a different company in the same field (115).
5. Conduct a series of five interviews with people who are relevant to the question this industry is resolving.
6. Write a blog post or short research paper mapping this industry.

7. Attend three different events that are hyperspecific to this industry, seeking out the mavericks of this field (112).
8. Find a nonprofit that is approaching the problem from a charitable perspective and volunteer with it.
9. Convene a group of people who are thinking about this topic to discuss it and collaborate with.
10. Practice your ability to take a nonlinear approach by connecting the dots between an experience you have already had and this new mission.

WHAT'S NEXT?

→ Make a list of what you want to learn next (72)
→ Make a list of the companies you want to work for (119)
→ Go on a solo trip and contemplate your mission fit (40)

DECIDE WHEN TO
WORK FOR FREE

WORKING FOR FREE should not be your first resort. It can feel like progress—it comes with structure and responsibility, and you may learn something—but it also costs you more than just money. It costs you time and mental space, and most importantly it can change your perception of the value your skills have in the market.

It is a big decision. When you have all of this free time during a transition it can feel like your time is cheap and abundant. It isn't. There is endless work to do in pursuing lines of inquiry, in learning new skills (72), and in any of the fifty ways that call to you most. The reason we fall back on free labor is that it echoes the rhythm of a life that feels good—structured work. If you feel yourself being pulled that way, consider taking a stepped approach to changing your rhythm (57).

This is not to say that you should never work for free. The typographer, graphic designer, and lettering artist Jessica Hische created a flow chart entitled "Should I Work for Free?" that she made a print of a few years ago and I refer people to it often. In it there are only a few examples of when you should actually work for free as a freelancer—for your mom, for a nonprofit that you believe in that is not working through an agency, or for a friend who has donated an organ to you.

It is sarcastic and warm and yet holds a great deal of truth even for those of us looking for a job. Your value increases in your own mind first, and anything that influences the way you think about that value is worthy of consideration before saying yes for practical reasons.

THE EXERCISE

If you have the privilege and ability, there are certain times that working for free is worth considering. Before you decide to go down this path consider the following advice, which originally appeared in my first book, *Making Good*:

1. **Who are you going to be around?**
   Will the position give you access to a whole new world of contacts, or will you be spending your days with people you already know?
   If the job you are taking involves getting out of a cubicle, you may be better off. Whether it's representing the company at a trade show, helping coordinate an annual charity ball, or attending a conference, the ideal unpaid position should enable you either to get a broad survey of your industry's social landscape or to build one or two solid friendships with people already firmly established in your field.

2. **Will you be able to teach yourself what you need to learn?**
   Every job involves learning on the go. As a volunteer, you should know what you want to learn from this experience and drive your own education. If, for example, having access to the company's internal workings will allow you to learn something worthwhile, then working for free can be highly valuable.

3. **What is your exit plan?**
   "I hope they will hire me after my internship" doesn't count as a career plan. Do you want to be introduced to a key player at a part-

ner organization? Do you want to make contacts? Find funding? If you know what you want at the outset of your unpaid position you can work toward it right away.

Volunteering is different from working for free. Remember, just because a business may not make money, that doesn't mean it is a nonprofit. Volunteering should be reserved for nonprofit organizations and causes. The motivation and the opportunities can still be judged by the factors above, but these can be overridden at any time by your desire to make a difference. Volunteering can also function as a more temporary way to make a stepped rhythm change (57), to build your sense of mission (194), or to learn about a particular industry's nonprofit counterpart.

WHAT'S NEXT?

→ Download your bank statement and discover how long your money will last (12)
→ Reduce your costs and live with less (162)
→ Commit to doing these four things when you feel overwhelmed (47)

WRITE YOUR OWN JOB DESCRIPTION

THIS IS AN EXERCISE you should do only if you are asked to. If you haven't been asked yet, skip this chapter. Being asked to write your own job description is an opportunity to get the job you have never heard about but have always wanted. In nonlinear careers it happens more commonly than you may expect, especially with young companies, start-ups, and nonprofits.

You will be meeting with an old mentor (112) or someone you've identified at a company you want to work with (119), and the conversation will turn to working together. This person will turn to you and ask, "Will you write your job description for me and then let's discuss it and try to find a way to work together." This is the prime opportunity, and yet it can be terrifying.

Questions abound: What if I get it wrong? What does the company need? What do I need from my professional situation? Am I just importing the things that I didn't like from my last job into this job description because I think they have to be there? What is flexible? Why would the company want this job done and what would its ideal outcomes be? What are mine? Do they line up? How does this feel?

To begin parsing through these questions and the others that are unique to your opportunity, it is important to remember that this is a great sign. This is a privilege. The person you talked to wants to work with you to find something that is mutually beneficial. Now you are on the same side of the table, so treat this exercise as a conversation, not a perfect report ready for grading.

THE EXERCISE

There are three main stages to go through when writing your job description. The first is getting the information you need. The second is reconciling your path with the employer's desires. And the third is framing the conversation.

Stage 1: Getting the Information

The major questions to address at this stage are:

How would your work move the company's work forward?
Which budget would your job come from?
Is the job nested under marketing operations or business development function?
What are the expectations the employers have from this job?
What isn't currently getting done that they would hope you would do?
To whom would this job report?
What resources would you have to manage, allocate, and access during this job?
Do competitors have similar jobs posted? What is included in their job descriptions?

You should be able to find most of the answers to these questions through your initial conversations and/or through publicly accessible information on the company's website. You don't need to be 100 percent correct—just in the ballpark. They will inform the needs and the reasons the firm would want to hire you. If you need additional information, it is best gathered in a casual conversation instead of an e-mail with a list of questions. You want to keep as much of the work on your plate as you can so that you don't overwhelm your potential employer. If you are unsure of how to answer why the company would be incentivized to hire a person like you, seek out people that are familiar with the industry or have worked at competitors and ask them. The more information you can gather about the firm's motivations from any and all sources, the better you will be at framing your job description.

Stage 2: Your Path, Their Needs

The second stage of writing your own job description involves understanding what your ideal job looks like, knowing what path you want to walk, and figuring out how to structure your job description so you are helping the company achieve its needs without taking you off your path. To figure this out you may need to describe your dream job (31) or write fiction about yourself (37).

Ask yourself the following questions:

What do I need from the company to deliver on the above?
What am I dependent on?
How could focusing on my ideal way of working help me do this job better? Structurally, how would this change the job description? For example, does it mean three days a week, does it mean working from home one day a week, does it mean having the ability to take people out for lunch?

The assumptions you have about how you should work, which are shaped by your previous experiences, come into play most acutely at this stage of the process. As mentioned previously in regard to taking a vacation buffer (8), it is easy to re-create the structure of a job you have had previously regardless of whether you liked it or not—especially when writing your job description. Remember, there are no right ways to get work done, but there is work to be done and results to show. Your goal is to write a job description that is grounded in what the employer's needs are and then walk backward, showcasing how you would deliver that work. Consider the following two methods of writing a job description with location-flexible employment as the goal:

The Self-Centered Method

- ❐ I will create a content strategy and manage social media accounts.
- ❐ I would like to work from home Mondays, Wednesdays, and Fridays.

The Company-Centered Method

- ❐ Deliver a content strategy and ongoing social media management that builds an audience by 50 percent and generates sales.
- ❐ Conduct field research and keep flexible working hours and location, ensuring that social media is an always-on function.

The company-centered job description leaves room for discussion, it's grounded in the company's goals, and it promises what you can deliver, all while leaving you permission to work from home. The main thing the employer will be looking for in the job description is that you can deliver on the goals. How you reach these goals and how you live your life while you do it is up to you.

Stage 3: Framing the Conversation

Before you present your job description, consider how you frame the conversation. In your e-mail, be explicit with the firm that this is the start of a conversation, a draft that you are open and looking forward to discussing.

Where applicable, write your job description in bullet points. Each bullet point will become a point of discussion when you walk through the document together.

During the conversation try to spend the majority of the time listening. Pay attention to what points the employers are interested in, which ones they skip over, and which ones they elaborate on. Tell them that you want to do another draft, and after the meeting incorporate their feedback and send the next draft of the job description to them as soon as possible. The more verbatim language you can incorporate into the second draft of the job description, the better.

When dealing with smaller companies for whom creating a new job means taking a risk, offer to write a ninety-day plan covering what you would do in your first days at the company. Taking this approach and potentially pitching yourself as a ninety-day contract (at least initially) instead of as a full-time employee from the start gives you more power and lowers the risk for them. This makes it easier for them to say yes and for you both to get a sense of the working relationship.

WHAT'S NEXT?

→ Talk to a recruiter and ask about his or her experience hiring for your ideal job description (173)
→ Decide how much you need to make before you go into an interview (212)
→ Make your own finish line and celebrate how far you have come (139)

CHANGE YOUR
DECISION-MAKING METHOD

THE FINAL AND MOST IMPORTANT moment of the job search is deciding which job to take. The average adult makes thirty-five thousand decisions a day, and yet we rarely investigate the process of how we do this. This becomes especially important as a person begins to make the dozens of small decisions that lead up to the major question "Where should I work next?"

We develop our decision-making methods during the early years of our lives, and they often go unexamined. They include strategies like making a pros and cons list; trusting our gut; talking it through with a friend, adviser, or mentor; analyzing numbers or outcomes; looking for a sign; or going on emotion. Sometimes it is a combination of these as we try to find the right method for the right problem—building enough conviction to decide yes or no. This exercise is about becoming a more flexible decision maker so you are able to access alternative answers you wouldn't have considered previously.

Daniela Plattner first taught me the concept of "embodied decision making." She is a dancer, a facilitator, and a coach who has championed embodied decision making for many audiences and clients, ranging from the Wanderlust Yoga Festival to Fortune 500 companies.

Embodied decision making is the act of looking to our bodies and movement as a way of learning and generating insights. It relies on the belief that our bodies hold wisdom that we don't often verbalize and don't listen to. In order to access this knowledge, we need to learn to ask a question, move, and find answers in our bodies.

When I met Daniela, she gave me an exercise to do in order to experience what embodied decision making felt like. She asked me for a question that I was actively dealing with. I told her I was trying to decide whether to go back to Toronto or to stay and continue writing where I was.

She told me to ask my throat.

I wasn't quite sure what she wanted me to do. Ask my throat—okay, I thought. Throat—what should I do?

"It says I should say what I feel," I said rather quickly to just sort of continue the conversation. I figured I got it and it wasn't for me. I probably was not going to use this decision-making method anytime soon.

But she could tell and stopped me. "Try again—actually slow down, breathe slower and deeper than you were a second ago, and write a dialogue in your notebook. Have a conversation with your throat."

So I did. I began giving my throat a voice:

ME: So what should I do? Should I head to Toronto? It will be fun.
THROAT: You know that is a short-term gain that you are going to regret later. You did want to work, right?
ME: But I can work there.
THROAT: You are just moving for the sake of moving. You are calm here. You should stay.

I was surprised by my throat's insistence—or my body's insistence. I knew I was thinking of moving for the sake of moving, but I had really not given any thought or weight to that idea until I had a conversation with myself about it. I felt surprised at how clearly that inner voice was telling me that I shouldn't go.

Daniela explained that I could take it one step further, consulting different parts of my body—different parts having different voices and holding different types of knowledge. The more we begin to listen, the more character, the more strength, and the more voice we have to draw on.

We have thousands of opportunities each day to practice alternative decision-making methods. It starts with the small decisions; these can be as simple as deciding what to eat for lunch. Slowly, as we build our repertoire and confidence, we will naturally become flexible decision makers, choosing the right decision-making method for those high-pressure moments with certitude and confidence.

THE EXERCISE

1. **List your current decision-making methods.**
   Make a list of all the ways that you currently make decisions. These could include steps that were listed above, like making a pros and cons list, talking it through with a friend, or going on intuition. Make note of the methods you rely on most regularly.

2. **Choose a decision.**
   Choose a decision that feels alive for you right now. It can be helpful to practice with simple everyday decisions when you are testing new methods for the first time. There are thousands to choose from each day. For this exercise pick just one.

3. **Try different methods.**
   Try using at least three different methods to answer the same question. Consider how the methods determine the outcome and what different information you pay attention to for each method.

4. **Practice embodied decision making.**
   As a way of stretching yourself creatively and seeing just how different your answers can be, based on which decision-making method you use, try embodied decision making. Pause, slow down your

breathing, pose a question, and have a dialogue with your body. You can write this out in your journal like a script or just listen inside— you might hear answers in words, feelings, sensations, or images.

WHAT'S NEXT?

→ Switch plans completely (158)
→ Practice making decisions by choosing three events to attend (122)
→ Decide how much money you need to make (212)

START WORK WITHOUT TELLING THE COMPANY

THIS IS, admittedly, a bit of a gamble. I would try all the other steps before this one, but if you are the type of person who is bold, takes risks, and isn't afraid of failure, then this may be for you.

I first heard about new graduates starting to do work without telling the company in the start-up world. The start-up world has a culture that prides itself on rewarding unorthodox methods and behaviors that show an "all hands on deck" approach. So be cautious and know that this doesn't work for every industry. For example, it doesn't necessarily make sense to start presenting an operations plan for a company without actually knowing the information you need to create one, nor does it make sense to start doing work if you are ten or more years into your career and an in-demand executive looking for a new job. Trust yourself and use common sense.

This type of proactive pitching is more common in the advertising world. Agencies will pitch briefs and ideas "on spec" with the hopes that it will win them a client or a new campaign. Why can't you?

THE EXERCISE

These are a few ground rules that will increase your chances of getting an interview and getting the job you want.

1. Choose a project that is small and manageable and get to work. Companies want to know you are proactive, not desperate. For your own sanity, make sure that the project you take on demonstrates your skill and takes under five hours to complete.

2. Ground the project in a hard skill. This is not the time to demonstrate your leadership abilities. This exercise works only if you ground the project in a hard skill that the company needs and that is related to the job the company is hiring for. Do you want to work as a marketing manager? Run one Facebook ad, and show the firm the different tests, results, and methods you used to optimize the traffic. If you want to work in human resources, choose an open position and send the firm a lead list of candidates that you sourced, with an explanation of how you chose them, explaining why you want to do this work in-house.

3. Make sure you pick something you know you can do well. If you are leading with your work, you have to be good. This is not the time to practice learning something new. You will be judged based on what you produce, so make sure it is relevant and up to the company's standards.

4. Send an e-mail to the CEO or a high-level employee telling what you did and that you are committed to working with the company. Adapt a version of the e-mail that will get you the job (184).

5. Don't expect a response. Read the chapter on creating a job search spreadsheet (170). A company doesn't owe you a response no matter how much work you put in. The more preparation and actual work you put in, the easier it is to forget this fact and expect the company to hire you. Take a second look at your job search spreadsheet to

remind yourself of all the options you have, instead of getting too focused on just one.

WHAT'S NEXT?

→ Decide when to work for free (198)
→ Go to a job board and then leave (167)
→ Instead of helping a company, try helping five people in your network (102)

FIELD NOTE: DECIDING HOW MUCH YOU NEED TO MAKE

In the 1970s, renowned sociologist Amitai Etzioni surveyed Americans, asking whether growth was a good thing. At that time, less than fifty years ago, 69 percent of the population were either highly uncertain or antigrowth. Today the question isn't even asked. Growth is presumed to be the only answer. We no longer stop and ask ourselves what is enough.

The question "How much is enough?" yields a drastically different answer for each individual. Your answer, like mine, will depend on a multitude of external and internal realities and beliefs that you have been accumulating throughout your life. When it comes to your ideal salary, the answers are deeply personal. There is no one amount. There are studies that show that happiness levels out after $75,000, but a measure of happiness doesn't account for our subjective personal lives—it doesn't account for what we grew up with, what our understanding of money is, where we came from, where we live, and our evolving emotional relationship to money.

These questions are personal. This doesn't mean you shouldn't be aware of what your value is—that you shouldn't be a tough negotiator.

There are some rules of thumb worth knowing, like you should always ask for 20 percent more if you are moving from one company to another and you should do objective research at websites where people anonymously report their salaries, but these steps stand somewhat apart from the question of how much *you* need to make. What is enough for you?

The organization Resource Generation has amazing programming and materials on the concept of "enough." The group's mandate is to help those with privilege (largely financial) to leverage it for social change, to create a new generation of philanthropists who support grassroots organizing. The training materials pose a number of questions (some of which are included below) that are worth considering, regardless of your financial background or how much money you grew up with.

One of the premises is that our stories around money didn't appear in a vacuum. They were informed by both lessons we were taught and actions we witnessed by our families, by our culture, and by the communities we grew up in. Going back and investigating where your understanding of money came from can be telling. This can also be a powerful exercise to do with a partner. There isn't one "right" money story. They are all different whether you have a lot or grew up with very little, and yet they shape how you think about savings, how you think about debt, what you think happens when you have a lot of money, and what it means to live with less (162).

If we don't decide to pay attention to the stories that shape us, we simply re-create the stories that we were given. If we choose to look and examine, then we are giving ourselves a choice about whether these are the stories we want to live with.

In his book *The Wayfinders*, Wade Davis discusses a conversation he had with a Tibetan lama. "Western science and efficiency has made a major contribution to minor needs," he said. "We spend all of our lifetimes trying to live to be a hundred without losing our hair or teeth. The Buddhist spends his lifetime trying to understand the nature of existence." It is important to ask yourself what you are focused on, what you are working toward, and why. Why do you want more money? What will spending enable you to find out or answer? How much is enough? What you concentrate on determines what you need.

This may sound therapeutic or repetitive or like a bit of a letdown if you were looking for a chapter that told you that you deserve $100,000 tomorrow, but these are the questions that have been asked of others and that I have asked myself, and they are the ones you will have to answer to determine what is enough for you. Answering these questions gives you control and agency, and regardless of how much or how little the amount, they will give you an answer that will be the right one for you.

Either individually or in conversation with your partner answer the following questions to uncover what your money story is.

What lessons about money did your parents pass on to you?

What was unsaid but true about your family's relationship to money?

What has shaped your relationship to money today and how did that come about?

How much are your monthly payments, including student loans or debt?

How much do you need to pay in rent in order to be comfortable and happy?

On average, what do your friends make?

What do you feel a successful person your age makes?

How much money feels like enough? Where did that idea of enough come from?

How much money would feel like too little to you?

What kind of life do you want to live? Consider the three questions from the describe your dream job exercise (31) to help you decide.

What other pressures affect your earning potential? Which way do they drive your ideal salary figure—up or down? Considering these factors, what is that number?

What did you make at your last job?

What do people in similar positions make?

Discover how long your money will last (12) and create a long-term budget. How does this match with the answers to your questions above?

HAPPY

YOU GOT A JOB

CONGRATULATIONS! You have reached the end and another beginning. The excitement of walking in on the first day and the new possibilities of what you will build and what you will learn are waiting for you. You have found the perfect opportunity to put your new perspective and skills to work.

The process of navigating through these fifty ways doesn't ever stop. Many of the exercises are practices—ideas that you can consider at different times of your life—and they will continue to provide different answers. The job search process is a mirror of your life—it is a process of managing the buoyancy of the emotional ups and downs, navigating the yeses and noes, and working with the people and lessons that come to you in moments you least expect. It is constantly unfolding and nonlinear, and it demands work, a good type of work, which you have now experienced. Your body now knows the feel of this type of work. Congratulations.

I once saw a circus performance by a Swedish troupe called Cirkus Cirkör. It involved elaborate balancing acts, acrobatics, and narrative emotion woven throughout. The director, Olle Strandberg, wrote and created the piece based on his own story—he'd had an accident performing a triple somersault and badly injured his neck. The piece was called *Underart: Ode to a Crash Landing*. It was minimalist and beautiful. At the beginning of the show, a bearded man with the shape of a strongman of days past calmly walked to the center of the stage and began to speak. "Risk is what you take because I know and you know and who knows . . . questions can have different answers and so does risk. Circus is all about the risk and the risk is about this."

There is risk in pursuing a nonlinear career, and just as in the circus, risk can have different answers. It is not the easiest path—but if you are here and have chosen this path then it is your path and it is the right one. You have done it.

The exercises and the practices that are woven throughout this book are a testament to that life decision. They are a path for those like you who want to do the work, who have doubts but now know that they are enough. Who can ask tough questions, and won't settle for just any job but will pursue the career that speaks to them.

This is why the job you have matters. Your career emerges from the hundreds of small choices that you have already made during the course of this book. We each find our own nonlinear way and our own motivation for why we do the work we do.

You did it. This is a book about work but it is also a book about life. A book that if treated with diligence will leave you in the middle of a great career, with a job that is on your path, and with a few more experiences squarely aimed at answering the universal question of how a person should be.

Our careers and the questions they answer are lifelong pursuits. There is great work to do. Let's do it.

To learn more, sign up for the newsletter, and discover additional

resources that can help you navigate your nonlinear career,

visit us at www.50WaystoGetaJob.com.

ACKNOWLEDGMENTS

I would like to thank Julian Caspari and Chris Kang, with whom I had the pleasure of spending three years researching and understanding what it takes to navigate a nonlinear path. Our work together laid the foundation for this book. Thank you to the Ontario Trillium Foundation and specifically Arti Freeman for taking a chance on the three of us and giving us the support necessary to take the time to learn and let what we learned guide the project.

Thank you to Lindsay Edgecombe for believing in me, seeing the vision of this book through to the end, and helping it find its home at TarcherPerigee. Thank you to Lauren Appleton, my editor, and to Linda Kay Klein, Meaggy Aylward, and Mara Munro, my first readers, for providing commentary that was exactly what was needed. Thank you to both Heather Box for our enjoyable weekly calls while I was finding my story and to the Juxtapose team for being open to reading poetry, chasing down conspiracies, and understanding the importance of this book.

Finally thank you to all the friends who read drafts and supported the journey, without whom this wouldn't have been possible:

Jacqui Allen, Keleigh Annau, Miriam Bekkouche, Heather Campbell, Gita Drury, Lisa Griffiths, Alexandra Gugllelminetti, Alexandra Hammond, Douglas Holt, Simon Jackson, Mathias Jakobsen, Whitney Joiner, Jake Kahana, Faizal Karmali, Ed Keeble, Matt Kenny, Grace Kim, Albert Lee, Jacq Hansen, Billy Parish, Daniela Plattner, Jordan Puopolo, Sarah Ramey, Lodro Rinzler, Laura Schmalstieg, Jasmeet Sidhu, Molly Sonsteng, Sam Utne, Mimi Warren, Corey Wildnauer-Haigney, the Outspoken Agency—Tori, Tara, Catie—and my Arcosanti crew: Emily, Jerri, Hnin, Tom, Kendra, Joseph, Harmann, Erik, Laura, Fernanda. Thank you.

ABOUT THE AUTHOR

Dev Aujla is the CEO of Catalog, a recruiting and advisory firm that has provided talent and high-level strategy to some of the world's most innovative companies. For ten years, Dev ran DreamNow, a nonprofit design studio that builds products and programs that change the world. DreamNow has reached more than 500,000 people and raised millions of dollars for projects that do good.

Dev speaks regularly and has blogged for outlets that range from *Inc.* magazine to *Fast Company*. His writing and work have been featured in dozens of media outlets, including the *New York Times*, NPR, the *Globe and Mail*, CBC, MSNBC, and CBS News.

Dev holds an English literature degree from the University of Western Ontario and currently lives and works in New York and Toronto. In his spare time, Dev runs the Sorted Library, a small independent reading space in New York. He is the coauthor of *Making Good: Finding Meaning, Money, and Community in a Changing World*.

For more of Dev or to be in touch, visit: www.devaujla.com